Euripides
Hippolytus

D0743844

A new translation and
commentary by Ben Shaw

Introduction to the Greek Theatre
by P.E. Easterling

Series Editors: John Harrison and Judith Affleck

CAMBRIDGE
UNIVERSITY PRESS

CAMBRIDGE UNIVERSITY PRESS
Cambridge, New York, Melbourne, Madrid, Cape Town, Singapore, São Paulo

Cambridge University Press
The Edinburgh Building, Cambridge CB2 8RU, UK

www.cambridge.org
Information on this title: www.cambridge.org/9780521678278

First published 2007

Printed in the United Kingdom at the University Press, Cambridge

A catalogue record for this publication is available from the British Library

ISBN 978-0-521-67827-8 paperback

ACKNOWLEDGEMENTS
Thanks are due to the following for permission to reproduce pictures:
p. 3 Ashmolean Museum, Oxford; pp. 18, 31 © Bradfield College;
p. 45 Donald Cooper/Photostage; p. 49 © The Trustees of the British
Museum; p. 63 © Louvre, Paris, France/Lauros/Giraudon/The Bridgeman
Art Library; p. 72 © Louvre, Paris, France/The Bridgeman Art Library;
p. 98 photo © Maicar Forlag-Greek Mythology Link
http://homepage.mac.com/cparada/GML/; p. 106 James Fund and
Museum purchase with funds donated by contribution 10.185 © 2007
Museum of Fine Arts, Boston, all rights reserved; p. 117 © Continuum
magazine, University of Utah.

Cover picture: *The Death of Hippolyte*, 1860 (oil on canvas) by
Sir Lawrence Alma-Tadema (1836–1912), private collection/The
Bridgeman Art Library.

Contents

Preface

The aim of the series is to enable students to approach Classical plays with confidence and understanding: to discover the play within the text.

The translations are new. Many recent versions of Greek tragedy have been produced by poets and playwrights who do not work from the original Greek. The translators of this series aim to bring readers, actors and directors as close as possible to the playwrights' actual words and intentions: to create translations which are faithful to the original in content and tone; and which are speakable, with all the immediacy of modern English.

The notes are designed for students of Classical Civilisation and Drama, and indeed anyone who is interested in theatre. They address points which present difficulty to the reader of today: chiefly relating to the Greeks' religious and moral attitudes, their social and political life, and mythology.

Our hope is that students should discover the play for themselves. The conventions of the Classical theatre are discussed, but there is no thought of recommending 'authentic' performances. Different groups will find different ways of responding to each play. The best way of bringing alive an ancient play, as any other, is to explore the text practically, to stimulate thought about ways of staging the plays today. Stage directions in the text are minimal, and the notes are not prescriptive; rather, they contain questions and exercises which explore the dramatic qualities of the text. Bullet points introduce suggestions for discussion and analysis; open bullet points focus on more practical exercises.

If the series encourages students to attempt a staged production, so much the better. But the primary aim is understanding and enjoyment.

This translation of *Hippolytus* is based on the Greek text edited by J. Diggle for Oxford University Press.

John Harrison
Judith Affleck

Background to the story of
Hippolytus

Hippolytus was the son of **Theseus**, the legendary king of Athens who appears in several Greek tragedies (e.g. Sophocles' *Oedipus at Colonus*, Euripides' *Suppliant Women*). There are two accounts of Theseus' father. In Euripides' *Medea*, King Aegeus of Athens, on his return from a visit to King Pittheus of Trozen, visits Medea, where he seeks advice on his childlessness; in Trozen, according to one myth, he slept with the king's daughter Aethra, who later bore him a son, Theseus. The Trozenian version of the myth claimed that the father was the sea god Poseidon.

Theseus travelled to Athens at the age of sixteen to be united with King Aegeus. *En route* he began to forge a reputation for heroic deeds with the killing of notorious brigands like Sinis and Sciron (see lines 965–8, and Plutarch, *Life of Theseus*). At that time the Athenians were paying an annual tribute of seven men and seven girls to Minos, king of the island of Crete. These victims were devoured by the Minotaur, half-man, half-bull, which lived at the centre of the labyrinth in the palace at Knossos and was the offspring of Minos' wife Pasiphaë, who had been driven by the sea god Poseidon – angry with Minos for his failure to pay him proper worship – to fall in love with a bull. With the help of Pasiphaë's daughter Ariadne, Theseus killed the Minotaur and escaped.

Theseus took Ariadne with him when he left Crete, but abandoned her on the island of Naxos. Homer's version of this legend suggests that Ariadne met an early death on the island (*Odyssey* xi); according to others she became the consort of the god Dionysus. In some versions Ariadne's sister **Phaedra** was also abducted by Theseus. She later became his wife, bearing him two sons, Acamas and Demophon, who fought in the Trojan War. Theseus' return journey from Crete is famous for his failure to change his sails from black to white (see line 729). That led Aegeus to think his son was dead and throw himself into the sea that took his name: the Aegean.

After his father's death, Theseus became king of Athens and continued to enhance his reputation for daring (sexual) exploits when he conspired with Peirithous, king of the Lapiths, to abduct Persephone, queen of the underworld. Another of his conquests was Hippolyta, also known as Antiope, queen of the Amazons, a race of female warriors who fought a campaign against Theseus. Their offspring was the illegitimate **Hippolytus**, who was brought up in Trozen by the aged Pittheus, Theseus' grandfather. When Theseus went on to marry Phaedra, Hippolytus became her stepson.

Conflict later arose in Athens over the succession. The sons of Aegeus' younger brother Pallas, the Pallantides, tried to oust Theseus. He killed them, an act that required him to withdraw to Trozen to cleanse himself. As the play begins, Theseus has left Trozen to consult the Oracle at Delphi (perhaps regarding the pollution incurred for killing his cousins).

The surviving play, first performed in Athens in 428 BC, is the second treatment by Euripides of the story. The first – often called *Hippolytos Kalyptomenos* (*Hippolytus Veiled*) while the extant play is called *Hippolytos Stephanias* (*Hippolytus Garlanded*) – excluded the goddesses **Artemis** and **Aphrodite** and was criticised for the portrayal of a shameless Phaedra (see 935n). It must have had considerable impact as the comic poet Aristophanes alludes to the portrayal of Phaedra in his play *Frogs*, written at least twenty-five years later.

Later authors were also attracted to the legend: the Roman philosopher and playwright Seneca wrote a treatment of the story (*Phaedra* – see note on page 18) while *Phèdre* is acknowledged as the masterpiece of the seventeenth-century French neoclassical playwright Jean Racine. Both versions choose to focus on Phaedra's story, and while some variants are added (in *Phèdre* Hippolytus has an *objet d'amour*, the captive Aricia) both authors seem familiar with the extant play of Euripides. Although it is considerably less faithful to the original myth, Sarah Kane's challenging play *Phaedra's Love* (1999) is an interesting modern adaptation of the story.

Genealogical table

Early kings of Athens mentioned in this play: Cecrops, Erechtheus

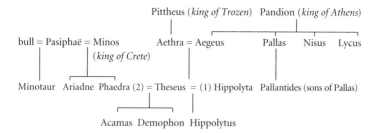

Select bibliography

Text

Diggle, J. (ed.) *Euripidis Fabulae*, vol. 1, Oxford University Press, 1984

Other text

Barrett, W.S. *Euripides: Hippolytos*, Oxford University Press, 1964

Texts cited

Fagles, R. (trans.) *Sophocles: The Three Theban Plays*, Penguin Classics, 2000

Watling, E.F. (trans.) *Seneca: Four Tragedies and Octavia*, Penguin Classics, 1974

Secondary

Craik, E.M. 'ΑΙΔΩΣ in Euripides' Hippolytos 373–430', *Journal of Hellenic Studies* 113, 1993

Dodds, E.R. *The Greeks and the Irrational*, University of California Press, 1951

Goff, B.E. *The Noose of Words, Readings of Desire: Violence and Language in Euripides' Hippolytus*, Cambridge University Press, 1990

Gregory, J. *Euripides and the Instruction of the Athenians*, University of Michigan Press, 1991

Lawall, R. and S. *Euripides: Hippolytus*, Bristol Classical Press, 1986

Mills, S. *Euripides: Hippolytus*, Duckworth, 2002

Morwood, J. *The Plays of Euripides*, Bristol Classical Press, 2002

Rabinowitz, N.S. *Anxiety Veiled: Euripides and the Traffic of Women*, Cornell University Press, 1977

Roisman, H.M. *Nothing Is As It Seems: The Tragedy of the Implicit in Euripides' Hippolytus*, Rowman and Littlefield, 1999

Map of Ancient Greece

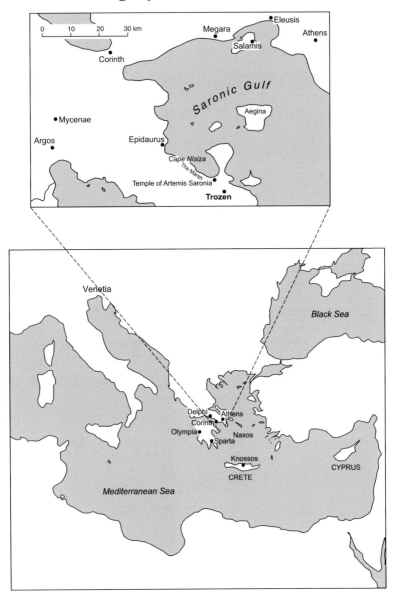

List of characters

APHRODITE	*goddess of love (also called Cypris)*
HIPPOLYTUS	*son of Theseus*
HUNTSMEN	*followers of Hippolytus*
SERVANT	*a member of the royal household at Trozen*
CHORUS	*women of Trozen*
NURSE	*Phaedra's attendant*
PHAEDRA	*wife of Theseus*
THESEUS	*king of Athens and Trozen*
MESSENGER	*one of Hippolytus' attendants*
ARTEMIS	*goddess of chastity and hunting*

PROLOGUE (1–117)

Euripides' prologues introduce elements of plot which explain the situation as the play begins. In *Hippolytus* the goddess Aphrodite, chief architect of the events of the play, delivers a prologue that predicts the future as well as explaining the recent past.

Setting

Hippolytus, produced in Athens in 428 BC, takes place in Trozen, a coastal town thirty miles south of Athens. The *skēnē* (stage building, see pages 122–3) represents the royal palace. In front of the palace are two statues, one of Aphrodite, the other of Artemis (both statues are directly addressed or referred to in the play – see 66, 98, 112 and 513). The Greek audience would immediately recognise a conflict of interests: Aphrodite stands for sexual love, Artemis for chastity.

Aphrodite

Aphrodite, the goddess of love, in this play is often called 'Cypris' (2) since she was first worshipped on the island of Cyprus, traditionally her birthplace. She represents sexual love, often denounced in Greek literature as an uncontrollable, destructive force that overrides rational, moral conduct (a view strongly expressed in Euripides' *Medea*). In *Hippolytus* Aphrodite is proud and vengeful, expecting all mortals to engage in sexual union to honour her.

3–4 Pontic sea / And Atlas' boundaries The Black Sea and the Straits of Gibraltar: the eastern and western limits of the known world.

6 I bring to the ground The Greek verb (*sphallō*) occurs frequently in this play (see also 97, 176, 253, 647 and 1398). The word was commonly used to describe the wrestling manoeuvre of tripping up an opponent. The metaphor is appropriate to an *agōn* (contest, see page 42) between gods and mortals.

10 Theseus' son For Theseus, see page v.

11 Pittheus the Pure The epithet of Pittheus, the former ruler of Trozen but still resident in the city (see 668, 765), hints at the sort of education Hippolytus may have received in Trozen.

12 the lowest of divine powers The Greek word *kakos* is difficult to translate (see also 75 and 73–5n, 420, 930, 933, 947, 1020 and note, 1060, 1065, 1067, 1295). It suggests both inferiority and wickedness. Although Hippolytus rejects sexual love as a corrupting influence, Aphrodite in her vanity takes his rejection as a personal affront.

APHRODITE Powerful and famed no less in heaven than
  Among mortals, I am called the goddess Cypris.
  Of all who dwell between the Pontic sea
  And Atlas' boundaries and look upon the light of the sun,
  I give preference to those who revere my power;   5
  Those who offer me proud thoughts I bring to the ground.
  For gods, too, possess this trait:
  They love to be honoured among men.
  I will soon demonstrate the truth of this:
  Hippolytus, Theseus' son, whom the Amazon bore to him,   10
  Educated by Pittheus the Pure, is the only citizen of
  Trozen here to call me the lowest of divine powers.
  He spurns the pleasures of sex and does not touch marriage.

Aphrodite riding a swan. Attic red-figure lekythos, c.440 BC.

Artemis

Daughter of Zeus and Leto (58), Artemis was primarily the goddess of hunting and virginity (see 15–17) – attributes attracting Hippolytus' devotion. She was also associated with childbirth (see 155–63). Like Aphrodite, she inflicted punishment on mortals who offended her: Actaeon was torn apart by his own hounds because he saw her naked.

16 his virgin Aphrodite resents not only Hippolytus' unusual chastity, but also his special relationship with Artemis.

20 wrongs Hippolytus has committed a wrong against Aphrodite. The Greek verb used (*hamartanō*) means 'fall into error'. Such an error (*hamartia*) against a divinity is usually the basis of a charge of *hybris* (see *'Hybris'*, page 40), a word often translated 'arrogance'. Aphrodite claims not to be concerned about Hippolytus' special relationship with Artemis (19), but his failure to acknowledge her divinity is a grave omission.

21 this very day In Greek tragedy the action generally took place within a single day (see also 53–4).

Theseus and Athens (24–35)

Theseus, famous for killing the Minotaur and his later attempt to abduct Persephone, wife of Hades, from the underworld, was a Trozenian hero, the son of Aethra, daughter of **Pittheus**. Later Theseus became the central hero in Athenian legend and was incorporated into the royal family as the son of Aegeus, grandson of King **Pandion** (24), and thus a descendant of the first Athenian king, **Cecrops** (32). For the benefit of the Athenian audience Euripides stresses Theseus' Athenian lineage, splices the traditions to make him king of both cities and uses his slaying of the **Pallantides** (33 – see note) to explain his absence from Athens. However, the Trozenian version is never forgotten, especially in the matter of the identity of Theseus' father (see page v, 42n, 1259n).

25 holy Mysteries Held in honour of Demeter and Persephone, the Mysteries were religious rites that secured safe passage to the next life for any initiated witness and involved a procession from Athens to nearby Eleusis.

25 Phaedra Daughter of Minos, wife of Theseus and stepmother to Hippolytus (see page v).

28–31 a temple to Cypris Aphrodite refers to her temple on the southern slope of the Acropolis ('Pallas' rock', 28) in Athens (see page 114).

33 pollution (Greek word *miasma*, see 306n) caused by shedding blood, especially of a family member, was considered a curse that could affect a whole city; **Pallantides** Theseus' cousins, who disputed his right to inherit the kingship of Athens from Aegeus (see page vi).

No, he honours Apollo's sister, Artemis, daughter of Zeus,
Reckoning her the mightiest of the gods. He is forever   15
Consorting with his virgin in the pale green wood,
Ridding the earth of wild beasts with his swift hounds:
The company he keeps is more than mortal.
I do not begrudge him these activities. Why should I?
But for the wrongs that he has done to me   20
I will punish Hippolytus this very day.
To execute the plan I set in motion some time ago requires
Little effort on my part. Hippolytus once left the house of
Pittheus for Athens, city of Pandion, to witness the rites of
The holy Mysteries. There Phaedra, his father's noble wife,   25
Saw him and was smitten in her heart by fearful desire.
All this was my doing. Before she ever came here to Trozen,
Phaedra built a temple to Cypris right beside Pallas' rock,
From where she could look out across to this place,
A lover pining for her absent love. Men will   30
Forever name the goddess's temple after Hippolytus.
Later Theseus left Athens, the land of Cecrops,
To escape pollution from the blood of the Pallantides,
And sailed here with his wife,
Consenting to an exile of one year.   35

Imagery of love

In line 37 Phaedra is tormented by 'pangs' (the Greek word *kentron* is used to describe bee stings, a horse's goad or any instrument of torture). Aphrodite goes on to describe Phaedra's infatuation as an involuntary 'sickness' (38). At 45 we learn that Phaedra is to die as a result of her love.

● How do these images of Phaedra's suffering underline Aphrodite's ruthlessness?

42 Poseidon, lord of the sea According to Athenian legend Theseus was the son of Aegeus. The earlier Trozenian legend had Poseidon as his father.

53–4 gates of Hades … this very day This chilling end to the speech adds a sense of urgency: death is imminent for the young man we are about to meet.

Review: the character and plan of Aphrodite

As she reminds us at the start of the play (1–6), Aphrodite has universal power because the effects of sexual passion are said to be felt by all mortals. When her pride is wounded she can use these same effects to destroy an individual or, as here, an entire family. There is a subtle malice to her plan of revenge. She uses incidental events in the characters' lives to ensnare them: Hippolytus' visit to Athens (23–5) enables her to cast her spell on Phaedra; Theseus' blood-guilt sends him to Trozen with Phaedra (32–5), where she cannot escape Hippolytus. Aphrodite's version of what is to follow generates intrigue and suspense: the audience are expecting certain events, but have no idea *how* they will unfold.

● How is Aphrodite characterised by her speech?
● How is her character appropriate to the force she represents?
○ How might an actor playing Aphrodite use tone and physicality to underline the character's message?

So now, in silence, the wretched woman,
Moaning and tormented by the pangs of love, is dying.
None of her household knows about her sickness.
Yet this is not the way for her passion to end.
I will bring it to Theseus' attention – all will be revealed.   40
This young man, my enemy, will be killed by his own father
With the curses Poseidon, lord of the sea, granted
To Theseus as a gift – three requests to the god
That would not go unfulfilled.
Phaedra, her honour intact, will none the less lose her life.   45
For I shall not think her misfortunes of more account
Than that my enemies should pay a price
Sufficient to satisfy me.
Now I shall withdraw, for I see Hippolytus, son of Theseus,
Has left the exertion of the hunt and now draws near.   50
Behind him walks a crowd of attendants shouting aloud
And honouring the goddess Artemis in songs.
He does not know the gates of Hades stand open,
And this very day is the last that he will see.

Hippolytus: first impressions

Hippolytus, returning from the hunt, leads servants and huntsmen in a simple hymn of praise to Artemis.

- How do these lines (55–65) create a striking contrast in mood with the previous speech (1–54)?
- How might a modern production use the stage space and lighting to enhance the contrast?

Dramatic irony

Dramatic irony arises when situations or words have a significance of which a character (usually the tragic protagonist) is unaware. Here Hippolytus places a garland on the statue of Artemis, neglecting to do likewise for the other statue on the stage.

58 daughter of Leto Leto, a Titan from an earlier generation of gods, gave birth to Artemis (see **'Artemis'**, page 4) and her twin brother, Apollo.

67 untouched meadow It is appropriate to the worship of Artemis that the garland is plucked from a wild, uncultivated meadow ('virgin' soil).

72 Modesty The Greek word *aidōs* is difficult to translate; it can also mean 'restraint' or 'shame'. It is the moral sense that inhibits a person's baser instincts and preserves purity. It is here personified as a gardener who protects the purity of the meadow (see 380–3 and **'A sense of shame'**, page 34).

Sōphrosynē 1

73 The Greek word *sōphronein* is here translated 'self-control'. The noun derived from it (*sōphrosynē*) can also mean 'moderation' or 'temperance'. The word is, however, used so extensively in Greek tragedy that it deserves to be thought of as having a wider sense (here conveyed by the translation 'virtue' in 74). Literally translated 'of sound mind' (like the Latin phrase *mens sana*), it often describes the 'good sense' to choose the right course of action in any situation and avoid the distractions of high emotion (see Index, page 128).

Self-control: taught or inborn?

73–5 Euripides' plays often contribute to contemporary debates about morality. Hippolytus' view of virtue was certainly controversial. In Plato's dialogue *Protagoras* (written in the 420s BC, at about the same time as this play), Socrates questions the standard Greek view that virtue could only be taught – a belief held by the Sophists (teachers of rhetoric who regularly visited Athens). Hippolytus, like Socrates, adopts the more radical view that to be truly virtuous one needed something like an instinct for good. Hence, Hippolytus considers virtue as something inborn and calls those who do not possess it in their nature *kakos* ('wicked', 'base' – see 12n).

HIPPOLYTUS   Follow! Follow! Sing of Artemis,   55
        Heavenly daughter of Zeus, who cares for us.
HIPPOLYTUS & HUNTSMEN
        Mistress, most revered mistress, child of Zeus,
        Artemis, daughter of Leto and Zeus,
        We greet you!
        Fairest by far of maidens,   60
        You dwell in mighty heaven,
        In your noble father's court,
        The house of Zeus, rich in gold,
        Fairest of maidens in Olympus,
        We greet you!   65
HIPPOLYTUS   For you, mistress, I bring this woven garland
I have prepared from an untouched meadow
Where no shepherd dares to graze his flocks
And no tool of iron has ever passed.
No, pure is the meadow through which the bee   70
Threads its way in springtime.
Modesty tends it with river springs
And only those whose self-control is not taught,
Whose virtue is complete and inborn,
Are permitted to harvest it; the wicked may not.   75

78 For it comes from a devout hand In Greek religion access to a holy place requires ritual purification from physical uncleanliness or contact with birth, sex or death. Hippolytus, however, believes that only those with no need for purification can enter the sacred meadow.

82 complete life's race The Greek verb means to 'turn the post' in a chariot race; a fitting metaphor for the horse-loving Hippolytus.

- Consider Hippolytus' belief that people cannot be taught to be virtuous. What are the implications of this view?
- What impression do you get from 66–83 of the nature of Hippolytus' worship and his relationship with Artemis?
- Hippolytus' prayer to Artemis could be interpreted as arrogant and pompous, or as devout and naive. Consider different ways in which the actor playing Hippolytus could be directed in this scene.

Hippolytus and the Servant (84–117)

In the last section of the Prologue, Hippolytus is accosted by an old man, a servant of the house. Low-status characters (servants, nurses, messengers) are common in Greek tragedy (especially in Euripides) and often express a more humble, superstitious view of the gods (the sentry in Sophocles' *Antigone* and the soldier in Euripides' *Bacchae* are good examples). Their cautious common sense often serves to underline the extreme or misguided views of the central character. The Servant is anxious that Hippolytus should show respect to Aphrodite and reconsider his exclusive devotion to Artemis. The ensuing conversation is conducted in *stichomythia* (line-for-line dialogue – an essential element in Greek tragedy, see 303–49n).

84–5 only gods must be called / Our masters The Servant's mode of address is pointed: although the Greek words *anax* ('lord') and *despotēs* ('master') are both used by slaves addressing their masters, only the latter is commonly used of the gods and the Servant's careful distinction is meant as subtle guidance to Hippolytus.

89 revere all alike

- What is the Servant hinting at in this phrase?

90 what proud man is *not* offensive? The Greek word (*semnos*) can mean not only 'proud' but also 'reverent' or 'pious' (see also 945), as well as 'haughty'. The Servant hinted (89) that Hippolytus should not be 'haughty' towards Aphrodite. By using the same word to describe Cypris as 'proud' (95), it is unlikely he would be directly insulting to the goddess. Rather, he is exploiting the ambiguity in the Greek in order to warn Hippolytus that if he fails to revere Aphrodite she could destroy him.

Dear mistress, accept this garland
For your golden hair,
For it comes from a devout hand.
I alone among mortals have this honour:
To accompany you, exchange words with you,   80
To hear your voice although I do not see your face.
May I complete life's race as true to myself
As when I began it!

SERVANT My lord – for of course only gods should be called
    Our masters – would you accept some good advice from me?   85
HIPPOLYTUS Most certainly. If I did not I would appear unwise.
SERVANT Well, you know the law that men have?
HIPPOLYTUS No, what law do you mean?
SERVANT The one that tells us to reject pride and revere all alike.
HIPPOLYTUS Quite right; what proud man is *not* offensive?   90
SERVANT There is some charm, then, in being approachable?
HIPPOLYTUS Very much so, and profit too, with little effort.
SERVANT Do you suppose it is the same among the gods?
HIPPOLYTUS It is, if we follow the same laws as the gods.
SERVANT Then how is it that you do not address a proud goddess?   95

97 Trip you up Another use of the Greek verb *sphallō* (see also 6, 176, 253, 647 and 1398).

Polytheism

Greek religion is polytheistic: different gods govern different aspects of life and all must be honoured. Conflict occurs between gods and men not only as a result of man's wickedness, but also through man's negligence (see 20n) as in Homer's famous story of the Calydonian boar, which was sent against King Oeneus because he failed to acknowledge Artemis in his thank-offerings for a bountiful harvest (Homer, *Iliad* ix). Hippolytus' concept of virtue or self-control (see page 8) requires him to be exclusive, but the Servant's warning (102) represents the standard Greek view of proper religious conduct.

110 As for your Cypris, I bid her a very good day Hippolytus' words are no more than a brush-off, a way of suggesting he does not want anything more to do with her. Hippolytus perhaps addresses this line to Aphrodite's statue as he walks off stage.

Review: the character of Hippolytus

Hippolytus' devotion to Artemis is very clear from the ritual of the garland and the hymn of praise. Yet the way he justifies his position with the contemptuous phrase 'revered at night' (101) reveals that his attitude to Aphrodite is far from neutral.

- What impression do we get of Hippolytus from Aphrodite's speech?
- Has this impression been changed, or confirmed, by his first appearance and subsequent dialogue with the Servant?
- Would you describe his attitude in the dialogue with the Servant as naive, confident or self-righteous?
- Is he a sympathetic character in the Prologue?

HIPPOLYTUS   What goddess? Take care your words don't
   Trip you up.
SERVANT   This one. Cypris who stands before your doors.
HIPPOLYTUS   Because I am pure I greet her from afar.
SERVANT   Even so, she is proud and renowned among mortals.   100
HIPPOLYTUS   I do not care for a deity revered at night.
SERVANT   My child, we must pay honour to the gods.
HIPPOLYTUS   Each of us, god or mortal, cares for whom we please.
SERVANT   Then I wish you good fortune – and better sense.
HIPPOLYTUS   Leave, men, go into the palace and see to the food.   105
   There's pleasure, after a day hunting, in a loaded table,
   And the horses need a rub-down.
   Then, after I've had my fill, I'll yoke them to
   My chariot and give them the exercise they need.
   As for your Cypris, I bid her a very good day.   110

111 humbly The Greek literally translates 'as is fitting for slaves to speak'. The Servant is thinking of his lowly status both as a slave and as a mere mortal in the presence of a powerful deity. His view that all men are slaves before the gods (see 84–5n) contrasts strongly with Hippolytus' attitude.

The attitude of the Servant

If Hippolytus interprets *sōphrosynē* as inborn purity (see **'Self-control'**, page 8), the Servant demonstrates the more conventional meaning of 'common sense' in his humility towards the goddess and his compassion for Hippolytus.

- How does the speech influence our perception of Aphrodite, of Hippolytus and of the Servant?
- If you were directing the scene, how would you make clear the contrast in status and attitude between the two human characters?

Review of the Prologue: conflict of attitudes

The Prologue of *Hippolytus* is complex, consisting of three short scenes which give a clear sense of the main conflicts surrounding the central character, Hippolytus. The audience has seen his extraordinary devotion to Artemis in the hymn of praise, but in light of the preceding speech, in which Aphrodite states her intention to punish him, this devotion appears a transgression (*hamartia* – see 20n) – an impression that seems to be compounded by his ensuing dialogue with the Servant.

- Assuming the statues of Artemis and Aphrodite are located on different sides of the acting area, how might the positions and movements of the characters (including Aphrodite herself) clarify their relationships to the two goddesses in the Prologue?

117 For gods should be wiser than mortals

- To what extent does the final line of the Prologue sum up the key issues in the play so far?

SERVANT   We offer prayer, humbly as befits our status,
To your image, Cypris, our mistress. Young men
Should not be imitated when they think like this.
Show forgiveness.
If someone in his youthful and impetuous spirit   115
Addresses you foolishly, pretend not to hear him.
For gods should be wiser than mortals.

PARODOS (ENTRY OF THE CHORUS) (118–69)

The Chorus, played by young men in the original production, consist of fifteen married women of Trozen. They enter from the town (conventionally to the audience's right), performing choreographed dances in the *orchēstra* (see Introduction to the Greek Theatre, page 123) and singing a formal ode – indicated by centred text in this translation (see also **'Lyric section'**, page 20). Unlike the audience, the women of Trozen – who see Phaedra as their mistress – are ignorant of the cause of her illness (125). With a natural sympathy they consider the likeliest causes of the illness: possession by a divinity (134–43), Theseus' possible infidelity (144–7), bad news from her native Crete (148–54), extreme pain caused by pregnancy (155–63).

A shift of focus

Euripides switches attention to the growing crisis within the palace at Trozen: in Theseus' absence, speculation about Phaedra's affliction intensifies as she grows increasingly frail. The focus shifts from the unconfined, outdoor, masculine domain in which Hippolytus is free to hunt and worship Artemis, to the confinement indoors of Phaedra, who must suppress her illness in order to protect her life and reputation.

119 Oceanus A mythological stream said to encircle the earth and thought to supply springs. The travel writer Pausanias mentions a spring at Trozen that maintained its flow throughout a nine-year drought.

122 a friend of mine In the first *strophe* (verse), the Chorus describe an everyday event: the discovery of a piece of gossip from a friend.

127 Hides herself indoors In Greek society the modest wife is expected to be confined to the *oikos* (house).

131 Demeter's grain In other words, bread. The goddess Demeter governed the fruits of the earth – corn in particular.

132 end The Greek word (*terma*) is used of chariot races. The lives of Phaedra and Hippolytus are described using this metaphor (see 82n).

134–7 It was a common belief that mental illness could be owing to possession by a god. **Pan** was thought to induce panic; **Hecate** was associated with sorcery and love-charms; the **Corybantes** were the ministers of Cybele ('mountain mother'), a goddess thought capable of inducing ecstatic states; **Dictynna** was a Cretan version of Artemis in her capacity as a goddess of untamed nature. Ironically, Phaedra's suffering is not caused by any offence *she* has given a god, but the result of Hippolytus' offence against Aphrodite.

142 the Marsh A large, shallow lagoon on the shoreline north of Trozen, separated from the sea by a long 'sandbar'.

CHORUS   There is a rock, from which, they say, water falls
           Straight from Oceanus;
    The spring flows into brimming pitchers,   120
           Flows forth from rocky crags.
Here, in the running stream, a friend of mine was
      Washing crimson clothes, laying them out
        On the flat of the sun-warmed rock.
From here the news first came to me of my mistress.   125

    She lies in her sick-bed, wasting away;
        Hides herself indoors,
      Fine linen shading her fair hair.
    This is the third day, I hear, of her fasting:
         She denies her body   130
          Demeter's grain,
    Death's unhappy end she longs to reach,
       Driven by secret suffering.

  Is it because of Pan, princess, that you wander
  Possessed? Or Hecate? The holy Corybantes?   135
       Or the mountain mother?
       Did you offend Dictynna,
       Goddess of savage animals?
       Did you neglect to offer her
      Libations of honey, meat and oil?   140
       It is she who roams here,
  Through the Marsh and over the sandbar,
  Among the watery currents of the sea.

Theseus the womaniser (144–7)

In his *Phaedra*, the Roman writer Seneca uses Theseus' attempt to help his friend Peirithous abduct Persephone to explain his absence from Phaedra. It is also a traditional element in the Theseus legend that as well as seducing Hippolytus' Amazonian mother, he abandoned Phaedra's sister Ariadne after she had helped him kill the Minotaur (332n, 333n). Theseus' reputation is hinted at here as the Chorus's speculation shifts from divine to human causes. The Greek for 'noble' (*eupatridan*) literally means 'of noble birth', but there may be a note of sarcasm in the Trozenian women's use of the word here (for more on Theseus' exploits, see page v).

146 Erechtheus' sons Erechtheus was a legendary king of Athens. His sons are the Athenian people.

149 Crete Phaedra's homeland (see page v).

159 heavenly Artemis In her capacity as a protector in childbirth (see **'Artemis'**, page 4). At 159–61 Artemis is addressed using the language of prayer – as if the Chorus, all of whom are to be imagined as mothers, are reliving the sufferings of childbirth themselves.

The Chorus. Open-Air Bradfield Greek Theatre production, 2000.

164 But look! The Chorus have focused the audience's attention onto Phaedra in preparation for her first appearance.

Review of the *parodos*

- What impression is given of the character of the Chorus?
- Would the *parados* be enhanced by allocating certain lines to individual members of the Chorus?

Has someone in your house seduced
Your noble husband,   145
Commander of Erechtheus' sons –
A union kept secret from your marriage-bed?
Or has some sea-farer
From Crete sailed here
To the harbour that offers   150
So warm a welcome,
To bring bad news to the queen?
Is it grief over her troubles
That keeps her soul bound fast in bed?

In the disposition of women   155
Is a malign, unhappy helplessness
Caused by labour pains and unreasoned thoughts.
The breath of it once rushed through my womb,
But I cried out to heavenly Artemis,
Helper of those in childbirth,   160
Lady of the arrows:
And to others' envy – thank the gods –
She always came.

But look!
The old nurse is at the doors,   165
Bringing the queen out of the house.
A dark cloud swells over her royal brow.
My heart longs to know:
Why is the queen's body so wasted, so pale?

FIRST EPISODE (170–515)

With attention now focused wholly on Phaedra, she is brought out of the palace on her sick-bed by servants and accompanied by the Nurse.

Conventions of outdoor/indoor

Women in ancient Greece were confined to the *oikos* (house) and had no public voice; they were under the authority of men who were anxious to preserve their reputations. Like earlier tragedians, Euripides challenges this convention by bringing his female characters into the public, outdoor domain (see 127n, see also *Medea*).

Lyric section (170–256)

Greek plays have a mixture of spoken and sung words. Other characters as well as the Chorus sing, and the Chorus (usually the leader) also engage in spoken dialogue (see 257n). This lyric section is chanted in an agitated metre (*anapaests*) that increases the urgency of the Nurse's enquiries and portrays the intensity and violent excitement of Phaedra's emotions.

176 you are down again The Greek word *sphallō* is used again (see 6n).

The character of the Nurse

The Nurse's first speech reveals not only her concern for Phaedra, but also her frustration at her inability to make a difference. While she undoubtedly cares for her mistress, her reflections on the difficulty of looking after an invalid (180–2) suggest a selfish motive for getting to the bottom of the matter.

- The Nurse refers to Phaedra as 'child' (196). What does this suggest about their relationship?
- How might the Nurse's philosophy influence the way she deals with her ailing mistress?

195 let my hair down to my shoulders The removal of her headdress shows a lack of modesty, breaking with conventional conduct for a woman in public. It perhaps suggests Phaedra's longing to submit to her desires.

NURSE	Oh, the evils mortals suffer! The pain of being ill!
	What do you and what don't you want of me?
	Here is the sunlight, here is your bright sky;
	Your sick-bed is now outside
	Because your every word was for coming out here,
	But soon you'll be hurrying back to your room:
	Soon you are down again
	And then nothing delights you,
	Nothing you have pleases you,
	You care only about what you don't have.
	It is better to be sick than to care for the sick:
	The one is simple, but with the other comes
	Heart-ache and hard work.
	Our mortal life is all pain,
	There's no relief from toil,
	Yet any better life beyond this
	Is shrouded in a dark cloud.
	We seem to long sadly for what is bright
	In this world, because we know no other life,
	Nothing is known of the world below,
	But we're swept along by idle tales.
PHAEDRA	Lift my body, hold my head up.
	I have no strength to support my limbs.
	Servants, take my hands, my lovely arms.
	This cap weighs heavy on my head –
	Take it off, let my hair down to my shoulders.
NURSE	Be patient, child! Don't thrash about like that!
	You'll bear your sickness more easily
	If you are calm and dignified.
	Mortals must struggle on.

Line numbers in margin: 170, 175, 180, 185, 190, 195

200 Ah! Phaedra's mind engages in wild fantasies and she seems unaware of the Nurse's warnings.

205 in front of others The Greek word (*ochlos*, see also 976 and accompanying note) suggests a mob of commoners. Even though Phaedra's words are only witnessed by the Chorus, the Nurse remains acutely aware of the impropriety of her conduct.

213 Thessalian lance A light throwing-spear used in hunting deer. Thessaly, a region of northern Greece, was famous for horse-breeding and hunting.

220 you could drink from there The Nurse is shocked by Phaedra's desire for hunting because it is predominantly a male pursuit. In her confusion she takes her mistress's wish to drink (201) literally.

221 salty Marsh See 142n. Phaedra invokes **Artemis**, perhaps clear in the knowledge of Hippolytus' reverence for her. Next to the Marsh, just north of Trozen, is a temple to Artemis Saronia (so called because of its proximity to the Saronic Gulf).

224 Venetia A fertile country at the northern end of the Adriatic, also famous for horse-breeding (see 714, 1117–18).

230 Which god is riding you now The Nurse reckons that Phaedra's distress is caused by a god diverting her from the path of sanity, much as a rider pulls the reins to alter his horse's course.

First impressions of Phaedra

As the royal wife of Theseus, Phaedra would be expected to behave with decorum in public – even in the throes of a severe illness. In the course of the play we discover that Phaedra values her reputation extremely highly (see **'Reputation'**, page 34) and yet she ignores the Nurse's advice and her first words are dangerously loose; she longs for activities – lying in the long grass, riding, hunting with hounds – that are not fitting for someone of her station. Her language literally conveys her desire to be with Hippolytus and metaphorically represents her desire for sexual union with him.

- What evidence is there in this scene that Phaedra's sickness is both physical and mental?
- How might the Nurse's ignorance of the cause of her mistress's distress bring a comical element to the scene?
- How might an actor playing Phaedra portray the character's frenzied excitement in 200–24?

PHAEDRA   Ah!   200
            How I long for a draught of pure water
            From a fresh spring! To lie and rest
            Beneath the poplars in the long meadow grass!
NURSE   Child, what are you saying?
            Don't talk like this in front of others;   205
            This outburst is sheer madness.
PHAEDRA   Then take me to the hills.
            I will go to the woods and roam
            Through the firs where hunting hounds
            Stalk and spring upon the dappled deer.   210
                     By the gods!
            I long to shout with the hounds,
            To hurl a Thessalian lance
            Past my fair flowing hair,
            To feel the grip of the barbed spear in my hand!   215
NURSE   Why so restless, child?
            How is hunting your concern?
            Why do you want water from the spring?
            There's a stream on the hillside
            By the city walls; you could drink from there.   220
PHAEDRA   Artemis, goddess of the salty Marsh,
            Of race-tracks echoing with horses' hooves,
            How I long to be on your plains,
            Taming the colts of Venetia!
NURSE   What mad words have you blurted out now?   225
            One moment you are off to the hills,
            Longing to set out for the hunt,
            Now you're on the sands and it's horses you want.
            We need a soothsayer, child:
            Which god is riding you now,   230
            Driving you out of your mind?

234 madness The Greeks explained irrational folly as inflicted by a god (the Greek *atē* covers 'delusion' and the 'ruin' it causes, see 265, 1131n, 1267n). Agamemnon (*Iliad*, xix) suggests he is not to blame for the madness that made him take Achilles' prize as Zeus and Fate placed *atē* in his mind. In Sophocles' *Ajax* the hero realises he has been driven mad by Athene. Phaedra has the same thought, and ironically her analysis is agonisingly close to the truth. Her fall as a result of this delusion recalls the wrestling imagery (see 6n).

235 cover my head again As Phaedra comes to her senses she remembers to maintain her dignity in public.

236 I am ashamed The Greek word is derived from *aidōs*, earlier (72) translated as 'modesty'. *Aidōs* can also be felt as 'shame' when it reflects self-awareness of a lack of modesty or restraint.

240–1 A good example of the tragic 'double-bind': Phaedra will suffer shame if she gives in to her desire and pain if she resists it (see also **'Reputation'**, page 34).

242 There you are The Nurse replaces Phaedra's headdress, restoring her modesty. Phaedra is silent for more than fifty lines.

Gnomic wisdom

Euripides' low-status characters offer general judgements (*gnōmai*) on the human condition (see 117 and 199), often helping to cast fresh perspectives on the principal characters' sufferings. In 244–51 the Nurse reflects on the suffering caused to her by supporting Phaedra throughout her illness; her feelings (like those of Phaedra for Hippolytus) are the cause of her present misfortune.

Excess and moderation

In another example of gnomic wisdom the Nurse uses the Greek phrase *to mēden agan* ('nothing to excess' – translated 'moderation' at 255), quoting the gnomic utterance above the entrance to the temple of Apollo at Delphi in central Greece. Moderation and self-knowledge were considered essential to keep favour with the gods.

253 trip us up The wrestling imagery used earlier (6n) was a metaphor for how humans are deceived by the gods. Its use here suggests that humans' principles may also be their undoing.

257 From this point the verse reverts to the iambic metre of spoken dialogue (see **'Lyric section'**, page 20). Having witnessed Phaedra's extraordinary state, the Chorus, probably represented by a chorus leader, approach to question the Nurse further.

PHAEDRA   I am cursed with misfortune! What have I done?
How far have I been driven from my wits?
I went mad, fell victim to some heaven-sent madness.
Ah, misery! Nurse, cover my head again –   235
I am ashamed at what I have said.
Cover me. Tears fall from my eyes,
They are filled with shame.
To be in my right mind is painful,
But this madness too is wrong.   240
The best thing is to die, aware of nothing.

NURSE   There you are. And when will death veil *my* body?
Long life has taught me many things.
The love that mortals share, one with another,
Should be moderate and must not reach   245
The spirit's inmost core.
Heartfelt love must be lightly worn
To be cast off as easily as it is drawn tight.
It is a heavy burden for one soul
To suffer the pain of two,   250
As I do for her.
They say that a life approached too strictly is
More likely to trip us up than bring us pleasure;
It is an enemy to good health.
So I applaud moderation rather than excess,   255
And many a wise man would agree with me.

CHORUS   Old woman, trusted nurse to the queen, we see how
Wretched Phaedra is, but the nature of her sickness
Mystifies us. We are ready to listen and learn from you.

NURSE   I don't know. I've questioned her but she won't say.   260

CHORUS   Not even how her troubles started?

NURSE   It's just the same. She is silent about everything.

265 madness Again the Greek word *atē* is used (see 234n).

269 She hides her suffering In the Prologue (22–31) Aphrodite mentioned that she cast the love-spell on Phaedra some time previously, when Hippolytus first visited Athens. It is therefore clear that Phaedra has been concealing her condition from Theseus for some time. Only in the last three days (264) has she begun fasting, and her sickness has clearly worsened dramatically.

271 He happens to be out of the country Theseus had gone to consult an oracle (see 762–3n). We never find out the reason (perhaps associated with his exile (32–3) from Athens, see page v), but his absence is dramatically convenient.

274 I have tried everything and got nowhere Although portrayed as a busybody who complains about the effort of looking after Phaedra (180–2), the Nurse is not merely engaging in speculation. She depends for her status and survival on her mistress's well-being and her enquiries are therefore urgent and motivated by self-interest (see also 249–51, 288).

279 My earlier words were unhelpful See especially 171–82.
● How successful is the Nurse in her attempt to be compassionate in 279–90?

281 that cannot be spoken of It was typical of ancient Greek society for gynaecological problems to be regarded as shameful. The women of the Chorus have already mentioned their experience in dealing with such ailments (see 155–63).

Sea imagery 1
291–2 Phaedra is described as 'more stubborn / Than the sea' which remains unmoved by any pleas addressed to it (in Euripides' *Medea* the heroine in her fury at being rejected by Jason is described as 'like a stone or wave of the sea'). The imagery is appropriate to the story: the Chorus later (729ff) refer to the fateful sea voyage from Crete that began Phaedra's misfortunes, and the destructive role of the sea god Poseidon has already been hinted at (41–4). See also 408n.

292 you will betray your sons Phaedra's two sons by Theseus, Acamas and Demophon (see page v). If she were to die in shameful circumstances the inheritance of Theseus' estate could pass to the children of previous or future wives (see 844–7).

294 Amazon queen Antiope or Hippolyta (see page v). The Nurse is well aware that the mention of another of Theseus' lovers could provoke a jealous reaction from Phaedra. The tactic works in an unexpected way, and her sentence is left unfinished.

CHORUS   How weak and wasted her body is!

NURSE   No wonder! This is the third day she has not eaten.

CHORUS   Because of her madness? Or is she trying to die?   265

NURSE   I don't know, but this fasting will kill her.

CHORUS   Your words surprise me – if her husband
    Accepts this state of affairs.

NURSE   She hides her suffering, denies she's ill.

CHORUS   Does he not guess when he sees her face?   270

NURSE   No. He happens to be out of the country.

CHORUS   Then you must try to understand her sickness
    And her wandering thoughts: can't you make her tell you?

NURSE   I have tried everything and got nowhere.
    Yet I will not let my efforts slip now. Stay here   275
    And watch how I treat my mistress in her distress.
    Come, dear child, let's both forget what was said just now.
    Don't be so tense: relax that gloomy frown and ease
    Those thoughts of yours. My earlier words were unhelpful,
    But I'll stop that now and try to give better advice.   280
    If your sickness is one that cannot be spoken of,
    These women here can help control it; but if your
    Misfortune can be made known to men then speak,
    And the matter can be referred to a doctor.
    Well? Why are you silent? You shouldn't be silent, child;   285
    Either correct me if I have said something wrong,
    Or, if I'm right, agree. Say something! Look at me!
    O dear me! Women, my work here is all in vain!
    I am back where I was before. My words failed
    To soften her earlier and she is not persuaded now.   290
    Well be sure of this, and then you can be more stubborn
    Than the sea: if you die you will betray your sons, for they
    Will have no share in their father's house. I swear by the
    Amazon queen, lover of horses, who bore a bastard
    Who thinks he's the true heir here, a master for your sons –   295

296 Hippolytus A moment of high drama. It is ironic that the Nurse achieves the desired reaction from Phaedra, but for reasons she does not understand. This is one of several examples in the play of words having an impact different from the one intended (see also 390–2, 635–8).

301 right mind The Nurse assumes that Phaedra's cry of pain (297) is for her children's sake and takes this as evidence of Phaedra's sanity.

303–4 storm of fate / That is wrecking me Language of sea-faring is again used as a metaphor for the perils of life (see **'Sea imagery 1'**, page 26).

Stichomythia (303–49)
In Greek tragedy passages of single-line dialogue change the pace and intensity of a scene. The Nurse has made a breakthrough and now increases the pressure.

306 defiled The technical term *miasma* (pollution) refers to contamination caused by murder, especially of a relative. Theseus had been forced to leave Athens because of it (see 33n) and the Nurse here wonders if Phaedra has perhaps been implicated. In Greece in the fifth century BC pollution and purity were generally held to be physical conditions, yet in this play both Hippolytus and Phaedra apply the terms to mental or psychic well-being.

308 close to me The Greek word *philos* (dear) can also mean 'relative'. Phaedra uses the ambiguity to conceal the truth.

313 my own mistakes Again the Greek word *hamartanō* is used (see 20n), though Phaedra is as conscious of her error as Hippolytus is ignorant of his.

Supplication
The Nurse clasps Phaedra's hands and knees in a gesture of supplication, a formal plea in which the gods are invoked as witnesses (refusal to answer the plea of a suppliant was punishable by Zeus). This strategy puts powerful pressure on Phaedra's already fragile sense of right and wrong (for a similar example of the power of supplication, see Sophocles' *Philoctetes*, where an obligation is placed on the young Neoptolemus to respond to the supplication of the crippled Philoctetes). By raising the stakes in this way, the Nurse makes the revelation of Phaedra's secret appear inevitable.

326 by speaking out The danger of words has already been highlighted (see 296n; see also **'Sophistry 1'**, page 40).

You know him well, I mean Hippolytus –

PHAEDRA   Ah!

NURSE   Does that touch you?

PHAEDRA   You destroy me, nurse! I beg you, by the gods,
Do not mention that man again.   300

NURSE   You see? You *are* in your right mind, yet you've no
Intention of helping your sons or saving your own life?

PHAEDRA   I love my children. It is another storm of fate
That is wrecking me.

NURSE   Child, are your hands clean of blood?   305

PHAEDRA   My hands are clean, but my mind is defiled.

NURSE   Has some enemy bewitched you?

PHAEDRA   No. Someone close to me is destroying me,
Against his will and mine.

NURSE   Has Theseus done you some wrong?   310

PHAEDRA   No! And may I never be seen to hurt him!

NURSE   Then what is this terrible thing that is driving you to death?

PHAEDRA   Leave me to make my own mistakes. I'm doing you no wrong.

NURSE   No, I won't let you. It will be your fault if I fail.

PHAEDRA   What are you doing? Will you use force on me?   315
You've taken hold of my hand!

NURSE   And your knees. And I won't let go.

PHAEDRA   Wretched woman! You will suffer
If you learn of these evils.

NURSE   What could be worse than not to get through to you?   320

PHAEDRA   It will destroy you. But what I am doing is honourable.

NURSE   Yet you conceal it even though what I ask of you
Is for your own good?

PHAEDRA   I am trying to find an honourable way out of
This shameful position.   325

NURSE   You'll appear more honourable by speaking out.

PHAEDRA   Go away, in heaven's name let go my hand!

328 the gift you owe me Phaedra's obligation to the Nurse as suppliant.

329 respect Again, the Greek word derives from *aidōs* (see 72n, 236n). In this instance Phaedra's sense of shame at her secret conflicts with her duty to be virtuous (see **'Supplication'**, page 28) and her decision to grant the Nurse's wish is made with great difficulty.

330 Now I'll be quiet We expect Phaedra to have the chance to explain her condition, but the Nurse's impatience prevents this and the *stichomythia* continues.

332 the bull When Minos, Phaedra's father, failed to sacrifice a bull sent by Poseidon to confirm his sovereignty, Poseidon made his wife, Pasiphaë, fall in love with it; their offspring was the Minotaur (see page v).

333 sister, Dionysus' wife Ariadne. Despite the help she gave him, Theseus abandoned her on the island of Dia (later called Naxos). She was rescued by the god Dionysus and married to him. However, Euripides may have in mind the version of the story in Homer (*Odyssey* xi), where it is implied that Ariadne was betrothed to Dionysus before she conceived her disastrous passion for Theseus (see page v).

338 back then In her current plight, Phaedra considers herself the third to suffer for love. Ironically, despite her ignorance of the cause, she is correct to assume that her love for Hippolytus has a deeper origin.

Review of *stichomythia* (303–49)
- In lines 303–49 analyse the different tactics used by the Nurse to apply pressure to Phaedra.
- What signs are there in Phaedra's words that she is weakening?
- What does the manner of Phaedra's eventual revelation (347–9) show about her feelings and condition?
- How might pauses be used to heighten the drama in 277–349 and especially at 329 (see note)?

Incest/Adultery
It is clear from the language (see 354, 361–2) that Phaedra's passion for Hippolytus is considered incestuous although they are not blood-relations. The story-pattern of the wicked wife attempting to seduce, and later destroy, the innocent youth is prevalent in myth: in the Old Testament Joseph is seduced by Potiphar's wife (Genesis 39) and in *Iliad* vi Homer describes the attempted seduction of Bellerophon by Antea. In contrast, myths describing male acts of adultery do not criticise or blame the adulterer. Even Theseus' involvement with Phaedra and her sister Ariadne (see 333n and **'Theseus the womaniser'**, page 18) escapes explicit censure.
- In your opinion, does Phaedra's love for Hippolytus qualify as incest? If so, how does this affect our appraisal of her?

NURSE   I will not, as long as you withhold the gift you owe me.

PHAEDRA   Then I will give it. For I must respect your suppliant hand.

NURSE   Now I'll be quiet. It is for you to speak now.   330

PHAEDRA   My poor mother! What a terrible passion possessed you!

NURSE   For the bull, child? Is that what you mean?

PHAEDRA   And you, my poor sister, Dionysus' wife –

NURSE   Child, what is the matter with you? It's your own family
You're speaking ill of!   335

PHAEDRA   I am the third. How wretched my destruction!

NURSE   I am terrified; where is this leading?

PHAEDRA   My troubles began back then, not recently.

NURSE   I am no closer to knowing what I want to hear.

PHAEDRA   Alas.   340
If only you could say for me what I myself must say.

NURSE   I am no seer; I can't make sense of what is not clear.

PHAEDRA   What do they mean when they say people are in love?

NURSE   Something most sweet, child, but also painful.

PHAEDRA   Then it is only the pain that I am experiencing.   345

NURSE   What are you saying? Are you in love, child? With whom?

PHAEDRA   That man, whatever his name is – the Amazon's son –

NURSE   You mean Hippolytus?

PHAEDRA   It's your own lips you heard it from, not mine.

*The Nurse responds to the Chorus. Open-Air Bradfield Greek Theatre
production, 2000.*

The Nurse's reaction

- Earlier (244–6) the Nurse recommended avoiding strong emotion (see **'Excess and moderation'**, page 24). How successfully does she follow her own advice here?

357 this woman, this house and me The Nurse's loyalty to Theseus' family is evident. However, she also realises that Phaedra's desire has serious implications for her – loss of employment at the very least – since through knowing the truth she becomes an accomplice.

Review of 257–357

While the Nurse's pressing questions and supplication have played a major role in extracting the truth, there are perhaps other reasons for Phaedra's revelation. As the Nurse suggests (292–3), Phaedra's silence might not have guaranteed good fortune for her children.

- What features of Phaedra's conduct in 257–357 are dignified and noble?
- Could Phaedra have avoided making her revelation or was it inevitable, given the circumstances?

The Chorus's lament (358–69)

After her outburst the Nurse flings herself down in despair. In this brief interlude, as the terrible news sinks in, the Chorus offer a short lament for Phaedra.

- Compare the reaction of the Chorus to that of the Nurse. Which is more compassionate?

366 the hours of this day A reminder that the events of the play occur within a short time span (see 21n) and that Phaedra's revelation will rapidly lead to disaster.

NURSE No! What are you saying, child? You have ruined me! 350
Women, this is unbearable! I can't bear to live!
Hateful day! Hateful the light I look upon! I will fling
Myself down, let myself fall; I will die, be rid of life.
Farewell! I am no more if the virtuous have wicked desires –
Even against their will. Cypris is no god 355
But something more powerful than a god:
She has destroyed this woman, this house and me.

CHORUS   Did you hear? Did you hear
The unheard of, the pitiful agonies
The queen cried aloud? 360
I would rather die, dear woman,
Than have feelings like yours.
Ah, poor wretch to feel such pains!
What troubles we mortals suffer!
You are ruined, your misfortune exposed. 365
What do the hours of this day hold for you?
Some fresh disaster will befall this house.
Where the fate, sent by Cypris, is heading
Is a mystery no more, wretched child of Crete!

371 Pelops' land The Peloponnese. In mythology Pelops was the first king of this area of Greece.

Phaedra's view of human nature (373–86)

Unlike Hippolytus, Phaedra seems not to believe there is such a thing as innate purity (see **'Self-control'**, page 8). She believes people *recognise* what is right but that most lack the will-power to *act* on such recognition. Knowing her feelings for Hippolytus to be wrong, Phaedra assumes they stem from some weakness of will, and refuses to 'be swayed' (385) into absolving herself of responsibility for them.

A sense of shame: the two types of *aidōs* (378–83)

This is a notoriously complex passage. *Aidōs* (see 236n, 329n) is included in a list of 'pleasures' that interfere with virtuous conduct, along with 'gossiping' and 'leisure'. A 'sense of shame' might prevent virtuous conduct in the way that someone embarrassed or shy about acting might fail to do 'the right thing'. Phaedra then says that this sense of shame can be either good or bad – in a sexual context, for example (the Greek word for the genitals is *ta aidoia*), 'good' *aidōs* might mean modesty in bed while 'bad' *aidōs* might mean excessive inhibition or even sexual thoughts that stray outside marriage, like Phaedra's desire for Hippolytus. In other contexts 'good' *aidōs* might mean shyness about speaking out and 'bad' *aidōs* excessive inhibition in communicating (stubborn silence). In Phaedra's dilemma it is unclear which course of action is more likely to 'weigh heavy' on her family and she struggles to determine what is appropriate (382–3).

My first strategy ... / Next ... / Thirdly (389–96)

● Describe the three stages of Phaedra's plan in your own words. How different are the first and second stages (for 'self-control' the Greek word *sōphronein* is again used – see page 8)?

● At what point in the play did Phaedra fail with the second stage?

Speech and silence 1

In this play, words – spoken and unspoken – cause unforeseen difficulties. Phaedra, explaining her recourse to silence, claims 'there is no trusting the tongue' (390), especially when it 'speaks on its own behalf' (392).

● How do Phaedra's opinions on speech and silence reflect on her decision to justify her conduct in this speech (see also 329n)?

Reputation (397–8)

Phaedra shows concern about the opinions of others: suicide is the best way not only to overcome her passion but also to preserve her reputation.

● What factors might undermine Phaedra's attempts to preserve her reputation through committing suicide?

PHAEDRA   Women of Trozen, who inhabit this furthest shore of   370
Pelops' land, in the long hours of the night I have often
Idly considered how men's lives are wrecked.
It is not because they make misjudgements
That they do wrong – many who stray have good intentions.
The matter should rather be thought of as follows: 375
We know and recognise what is right but do not act on it;
Some out of laziness, others because they put
Pleasure before virtue. There are many such pleasures
In life: gossiping at length, leisure (a delightful vice),
And then there is a sense of shame. Of this last there are   380
Two sorts: one is no bad thing, the other can weigh heavy
On a household. If it were clear when each has its place,
The two things would not bear the same name.
Since these are the views I hold
I was not going to be swayed by any sort of charm   385
Into reversing my way of thinking.
I will tell you the course my thoughts took. When love
Wounded me, I searched for the best way to endure it.
My first strategy was to keep silent and conceal my
Illness. For there is no trusting the tongue, which knows   390
How to correct the thoughts of others but invites
Untold troubles when it speaks on its own behalf.
Next, I determined to endure the passion bravely,
Overcoming it with self-control.
But since I couldn't master Cypris by these means,   395
Thirdly I resolved to die – the best plan, no one would deny.
For just as I would not want my noble acts to pass unnoticed,
So I did not want my shameful ones made public.

400 as a woman As Phaedra is all too aware, Greek men in antiquity would be unlikely to interpret her predicament sympathetically.

401–5 Phaedra launches a scathing attack on 'the nobility' (the Greek word *esthlos* refers simply to those who are noble by birth), calling to mind examples like the adultery and shamelessness of Clytemnestra in Aeschylus' *Agamemnon*.

● Why is Phaedra so critical of the first adulteress?

406 The Greek word *sōphrōn* (the adjective from *sōphrosynē*) is translated here as 'chaste' (see '*Sōphrosynē* 1', page 8).

408 Mistress Cypris, born from the sea At this point Phaedra might turn to the statue of Aphrodite on stage. There is a myth explaining Aphrodite's birth as resulting from the foam (Greek word *aphros*) of Uranos' sperm. His son Cronos, Zeus' father, had cut off his father's genitals, which landed in the sea near Cyprus.

415 enjoying freedom of speech Phaedra pays tribute to *parrhēsia* (free speech between equals) which Pericles, in his funeral oration (Thucydides' *Histories* ii, chapters 35–46), champions as a fundamental privilege of Athenian democracy.

● How do lines 412–18 develop our understanding of the motives behind Phaedra's concern for her reputation (see page 34)?

420 When Time sets his mirror Time's mirror is a metaphor for the impossibility of escaping detection. In the simile that follows ('As before a young girl', 421), Phaedra again reveals her concern with external appearances: the mirror will eventually reveal blemishes, just as time will reveal the wicked.

Review of Phaedra's speech (370–422)

In this speech Phaedra has given a vigorous and dignified account of her struggles. Although bitter about her helplessness and how she might be perceived, she does not make excuses for herself and shows devotion for her sons in her reasons for contemplating suicide. While her feelings for Hippolytus have tested her resolve, she has at least attempted to show that her responses to her desire were reasoned attempts to recover her virtue – even if ultimately in the 'upright mind' (419) she considers the mainstay of a good life is lacking in her.

● How does Phaedra's speech evoke sympathy and admiration?
● 'Damned if she does, damned if she doesn't'. How might this be true of her decision to justify herself to the Chorus?

I knew my behaviour and illness were dishonourable
And that as a woman I was an object of hate to all men.   400
A curse on the woman who first disgraced her
Marriage-bed with other men! It was in noble families
That this evil first emerged among women.
When shameful deeds find approval amongst the nobility
Then their inferiors will find nothing wrong in them.   405
I hate a woman who presents herself as chaste
In what she says but takes shameless risks in secret.
Mistress Cypris, born from the sea,
How can they ever look their husbands in the eye
And not shudder that darkness, their accomplice,   410
Or the very timbers of the house might tell their secret?
This is what is killing me, dear women, that I may be
Caught shaming my husband or the children I gave birth to.
May they dwell in the city of the illustrious Athenians,
Flourishing as free men and enjoying freedom of speech,   415
Respected because of their mother. For knowledge of
His mother's or his father's sins enslaves a man,
No matter how spirited he is. They say the only way
To succeed in life is to possess a just and upright mind.
When Time sets his mirror before the wicked,   420
As before a young girl, sooner or later he shows them up.
I never want to be seen as one of them!

423–4 The Chorus appropriately praise 'self-control' (see 394, 406n) and these lines suggest they approve of Phaedra's efforts. However, there remains an uncertainty in the sense of *sōphrosynē* (see **'Phaedra's view of human nature'**, page 34).

● Which kind of *sōphrosynē* is most likely to secure a 'good name'?

Second thoughts

The Nurse's response to her mistress is carefully constructed. Ignoring the difficulties peculiar to Phaedra's adulterous case, she describes love as an irresistible natural phenomenon and attempts to show that Phaedra's refusal to give in to her feelings is both futile and blasphemous.

The power of love

● Compare the Nurse's words in 435–41 about Aphrodite's power with Aphrodite's own statement at the start of the play (1–6).
● What picture of love does the Nurse give in lines 431–51?

Examples from myth (442–6)

It was common to cite myths to reinforce an argument. For example, in Homer's *Iliad* ix, Phoinix uses the story of Meleagros and the Calydonian boar (see **'Polytheism'**, page 12) to underpin his warning to Achilleus. Here the Nurse does likewise, demonstrating to Phaedra the irresistible power of love with the stories of **Semele**, the mother of Dionysus, who died when Hera, jealous wife of **Zeus**, made her persuade him to appear in his elemental form as a thunderbolt; and **Cephalus**, whose marriage to Procris was ended against his will when **Dawn** stole him away.

● How appropriate do these examples seem to you?
● Do they strengthen or weaken the Nurse's argument?

CHORUS   Self-control is always to be admired.
The fruit it bears for mortals is a good name.

NURSE   Mistress, just now your misfortune gave me a   425
Terrible fright. But now I realise I was being foolish.
In mortals second thoughts are somehow wiser.
There is nothing unusual or difficult to understand
In what you've suffered:
The goddess has swooped down on you in anger.   430
You are in love – is that so amazing? Many mortals are!
And yet will you ruin your life for the sake
Of love? Then it's a poor deal for those who fall in love,
And to all lovers in future, if they must die!
When Cypris rushes on in full force there is no   435
Resisting her. She comes gently on those who yield,
But those she finds arrogant or proud, she takes
And treats with a violence you wouldn't believe.
She moves through heaven, in the waves of the sea,
And all things come from her. It is she who sows her   440
Gift of desire from which all of us on earth spring.
Those who possess the writings of the old poets –
All cultured people – know that Zeus once lusted
After Semele; that Dawn of the beautiful rays once
Snatched Cephalus away to the gods –   445
All because of love.
Even so, they don't avoid the company of the gods but dwell
In heaven, happy victims of their misfortune, I imagine.
Yet you can't put up with it? Your father should have
Conceived you on special terms, or under rulers other than   450
The gods, if you refuse to abide by these laws.

452–8 The Nurse presents a different argument: husbands and fathers will overlook sexual transgressions and the quest for perfection is fruitless.

- What do you think of the Nurse's use of gnomic wisdom (see page 24) in 456? Is it consistent with her position in 242–56?
- How effective is the roof simile (457–8) in explaining her point? Contrast her use of roof imagery with that of Phaedra (411).

459 a sea of troubles Again imagery to do with the sea is used to illustrate Phaedra's predicament (see page 26).

Hybris (463–4)
Hybris, here translated 'blasphemy', is overstepping a mark and knowingly or unknowingly challenging the gods – an offence punishable by *nemesis* (divine punishment, see 20n). These two concepts play a dominant role in surviving Greek tragedy. The Nurse had hinted at this argument earlier (449–51) but now uses the word *hybris* as a shock tactic.

- Which is the more obvious example of *hybris*: refusing to give in to passion as Phaedra does, or paying no more than lip-service to Aphrodite as Hippolytus does?

467–8 magic spells … sickness The Nurse suggests finding a cure, but she is deliberately vague: the 'cure' most favoured by Phaedra would remove her feelings for Hippolytus, yet this seems impossible. The alternative – to cure the 'sickness' by fulfilling the desire – is what the Nurse has in mind.

471–5 Like the jury in a court case, the Chorus see both sides, even though they still support Phaedra. While previously (423–4) they had praised virtue, they now suggest that the Nurse's 'practical advice', which could prove catastrophic to Phaedra, is more attractive to hear than any 'praise'.

Sophistry 1: fine-sounding words (477)
The Sophists, controversial teachers of rhetoric (see **'Self-control'**, page 8), boasted that in any dispute they could make the weaker (i.e. morally suspect) argument defeat the stronger, purely through well-structured, persuasive delivery. In his play *Clouds* Aristophanes describes how a son tutored at a school for Sophists can justify beating up his own father. Phaedra's description of the Nurse's words as *kaloi* (here translated 'fine-sounding') rather than *dikaioi* ('good' in the sense of 'just') recalls the contemporary debate about the worth of the Sophists (see also 490n).

Review of the Nurse's speech (425–70)
- How persuasive are the Nurse's arguments? Would you expect Phaedra to be convinced by them?
- Given the situation, are the Nurse's second thoughts wiser and more sensible than her initial reaction to the news (350–7)?

How many very sensible men, do you think, see that
All is not well with their marriages yet look the other way?
How many fathers help their errant sons in secret affairs?
To overlook what is not perfect is the way of the wise.   455
Mortals shouldn't work too hard at life.
After all, would you care whether every
Roof timber in your house was perfect?
You've fallen into a sea of troubles; how do you expect
To swim out? You are human, and if you've more   460
Good than bad in you, you are doing well enough.
Stop these wicked thoughts, dear child.
Stop this blasphemy. For it is nothing short of blasphemy
To wish to be stronger than the gods.
Have confidence in your love: a god has willed this.   465
You are unwell, but somehow turn the illness around.
There are magic spells and enchantments –
Some cure for this sickness will come to light.
It would take men too long to solve problems
If we women didn't find ways round them.   470
CHORUS   Phaedra, in your present misfortune
This woman offers the more practical advice,
But I reserve my praise for you.
Yet this praise is harder to bear than her words
And more painful for you to hear.   475
PHAEDRA   This is what destroys men's houses and
Their well-founded cities: fine-sounding words.
What is needed are not words that please the ear,
But a way to win a noble reputation.

480–1 fancy words … but / The man After Phaedra's response (476–9) to her attempts to persuade, the Nurse adopts a more blunt, direct approach.

483 you still possessed some self-control The Nurse turns Phaedra's view of human nature (see page 34) against her, suggesting that Phaedra's desire has robbed her of self-control (again, the word used is *sōphrōn* – see 389–96n, 406n).

● Is the Nurse's view that Phaedra is no longer 'a woman of self-control' a fair one?

Phaedra's determination

From the moment she confessed her love, Phaedra, summoning up her last reserves of energy, has spoken with dignity and conviction, to both the Chorus and the Nurse.

● How might Phaedra's act of confession have strengthened her?

Agōn

486 When two characters in Greek tragedy debate at length the rights and wrongs of a certain course of action, the scene is called a contest or 'challenge' (*agōn* – a word often used to describe political and legal debate in Athens' democratic assembly and law courts). The Nurse uses this word here, referring both to the challenge she faces and to the moral dilemma of the situation.

490 fine words Again the word for 'fine' is *kaloi*. Phaedra speaks ironically in describing the Nurse's words as fine (477, 493) when they are in fact 'terrible' (488) or 'shameful' (489) because they speak in favour of actions that bring disgrace. The Nurse on the other hand accepts that Phaedra's 'fine' (490) or 'fancy' (480) words are moral, but argues they are of no use. This ambiguity in the word *kaloi* highlights a further controversy in the debates of the Sophists: the conflict between words or actions that are intrinsically good and those that are good because they bring about a favourable outcome (see **'Sophistry 1'**, page 40).

500 a charm, a spell for desire The Nurse is deliberately ambiguous. She promises a remedy for Phaedra's longing, but it is not clear whether this involves removing the desire or consummating it (see 467–8n).

506 the two The Nurse means the charm and the token.

● What further ambiguities can you find in lines 500–6?

507–11 Though wary, Phaedra begins to show signs of capitulation.

● What evidence is there in these lines that Phaedra's energy and determination (see note above) to resist the Nurse are failing?

NURSE   Why preach? It's not fancy words you need, but   480
    The man. We must clear this up at once and speak
    The plain truth about you. If your life were not in such a state
    And you still possessed some self-control,
    I would never have led you on for the sake of
    Love and your own gratification.   485
    Yet now the great challenge is to save your life –
    This is no time for shying away.

PHAEDRA   What terrible words! Close your mouth!
    Do not allow such shameful words to pass your lips again!

NURSE   Shameful, yes, but they do you more good than fine words. 490
    Action, if it saves you, will bring you more advantage
    Than a reputation you'd proudly die for.

PHAEDRA   Go no further, in God's name! Your fine words
    Are disgraceful. My soul has been weakened by desire
    And if you make shameful acts sound fine then I will be   495
    Caught by the very thing I am now running from.

NURSE   If that's what you think, you shouldn't have
    Made your mistake, but since you have, do what I say.
    This is my next best offer:
    I have at home a charm, a spell for desire –   500
    It has just now come to mind. This will put an end
    To your sickness without dishonour or harm,
    If you have the courage to take it.
    We must get some item from the man you desire,
    A lock of hair or a strand of his cloak,   505
    And join the two to create a happy outcome.

PHAEDRA   Is this charm an ointment or a potion?

NURSE   I'm not sure. Don't ask, just let it help you.

PHAEDRA   I fear you will turn out too clever for me.

NURSE   Anything would make *you* nervous. What scares you?   510

PHAEDRA   That you might mention any of this to Theseus' son.

513–15   The Nurse turns to Aphrodite's statue.

- Why does the Nurse call 'Cypris' an 'accomplice'?
- Who do you think she has in mind when she says 'our friends inside' (see 308n)?

Review of the First Episode

After the lyric section (170–256), which revealed Phaedra's physical condition, and the Nurse's interrogation (culminating in the intense *stichomythia* of 303–49 and Phaedra's revelation), the remainder of the scene (350–515) consists of an *agōn* (see page 42), in which the two characters dispute the rights and wrongs of their situation. Although Phaedra has also been drawn into confessing her secret, her intentions are moral, while the Nurse's suggestions seem pragmatic and well meaning, but morally questionable.

Just as the Sophistic movement in Athens (see **'Sophistry 1'**, page 40) taught that the weaker argument could be made the stronger, so at the end of this *agōn* the Nurse's suggestions have prevailed over Phaedra's anxieties.

- Is Phaedra in any way to blame for her 'defeat'?
- What universal issues are raised in the formal debate between Phaedra and the Nurse?

Staging the First Episode

○ How might the physical weakness of Phaedra affect the physical dynamics of the scene? Would Phaedra remain seated on her sick-bed throughout the scene, or might she at least rise to address the Chorus (370–422)?

○ How might the physical reactions of the Chorus and the two central characters enhance the dramatic impact at key moments such as the supplication (315) and Phaedra's revelation (349)?

NURSE   Enough, child. I'll sort this out for you.
All I ask is that you, mistress Cypris, born from the sea,
Be my accomplice. As for what else I have in mind,
A word with our friends inside will be sufficient.   515

Phaedra and the Nurse. Royal Shakespeare Company, London, 1979.

FIRST *STASIMON* (516–45)

A *stasimon* is the term given to the choral song that comes at the end of an episode. Verses in a *stasimon* are made up of balanced pairs, consisting of a *strophe* followed by an *antistrophe*.

The Nurse leaves to carry out her plan, leaving an anxious Phaedra on stage with the Chorus. They sing of Eros, a powerful deity (516–23) and one who must be honoured as highly as the mighty Olympians (524–31). Eros is the agent of Cypris, whose destructive power is emphasised in the mythic examples of Iole (532–8) and Semele (539–45).

Eros (516–23)

Imagined as both the bringer of desire and desire itself, Eros is far more sinister than later representations in classical art of a mischievous Cupid and his arrows. After the reference to 'sweet delight', the Chorus, no doubt uneasy about the Nurse's plan, focus on the malice of Eros, a 'tyrant over men' (528) and bringer of war whose attacks are sudden and violent. Euripides even invents a formidable parentage: Eros is 'child of Zeus'.

- Compare the portrayal of Eros in this *stasimon* with the impression of love presented by Aphrodite and the Nurse.

A cautionary note (524–31)

The Chorus warn that it will be futile ('in vain' – see 1348n) for the people of Greece ('Hellas') to sacrifice 'cattle' for major cults – such as Zeus at Olympia (site of the ancient Olympic Games, located by the river Alpheus), and Apollo at Delphi (the famous oracle, located in the Pythian temple) – if they ignore the equally powerful Eros. There is little evidence of any cult worship of Eros in fifth-century BC Athens.

529 Holder of the keys to Aphrodite's sweet bridal beds

- Is this an effective metaphor?

Iole (532–8)

Iole, daughter of Eurytus, king of Oechalia, was promised as a bride to whoever defeated her father in an archery contest. When Heracles ('Alcmene's son') was victorious, Eurytus refused to hand over the prize. Heracles therefore sacked the city and stole Iole away.

535 running bacchant nymph Vase paintings often depict beautiful nymphs running away from lecherous satyrs (half-man, half-goat). Here Iole is described both as 'bacchant', a worshipper of Bacchus (see **'Semele'**, page 48), possessed by a kind of madness, and also as 'Yoked', a word used to describe the harnessing of beasts of burden and here highlighting Aphrodite's power – over both Heracles and Iole – to inflict sexual servitude.

CHORUS	Eros, Eros, you pour desire on the eyes,
	Bringing sweet delight in the soul
	Of those against whom you campaign.
	May you never come with trouble for me,
	May you never appear at the wrong time.	520
	Stronger than shafts of fire or starlight
	Are the arrows of Aphrodite,
	Fired from the hands of Eros, child of Zeus.
	In vain, in vain, by the streams of Alpheus,
	And Apollo's Pythian temple,	525
	Does the land of Hellas
	Pile high the heaps of slaughtered cattle
	If we do not honour Eros, tyrant over men,
	Holder of the keys to Aphrodite's sweet bridal beds,
	Who visits devastation on men when he comes,	530
	Propelling them through all misfortunes.
	The girl of Oechalia, a filly still unbroken,
	Was unwed, had never known a man –
	But Cypris took her from Eurytus' home,
	Yoked her like a running bacchant nymph,	535
	Gave her to Alcmene's son
	Amid blood, amid smoke –
	Murderous marriage! Wretched bride!

Semele (539–45)

The second *antistrophe* gives a further example of Cypris' malevolent power. Thebes was the birthplace of the god Bacchus, called 'twice-born' because he was removed from the womb of his mother (Semele) and stitched into Zeus' thigh for the remainder of gestation. At the same time, Semele was killed by Zeus' 'flaming thunderbolt' when Zeus' wife Hera, in her jealousy, persuaded her to ask him to appear in his true form. The Nurse had earlier (see 443–4 and note) used the example of Semele to persuade Phaedra to yield to her desires.

539 spring of Dirce The Chorus call upon famous landmarks in Thebes to bear witness to the terrible fate of Semele. The theme of violence resulting from passion is maintained however, since Dirce was killed because of her role in the torture of Antiope (*not* the mother of Hippolytus), a Theban princess pursued and raped by Zeus.

545 darts about like a bee This image may seem tame in comparison with the earlier descriptions of the fearsome Cypris. However, it reveals the unpredictability of the goddess who, as this *stasimon* shows, picks victims at will (for further instances of bee imagery see **'Imagery of love'** on page 6 and 70–1).

Victims of violence

The second strophic pair switches attention to Aphrodite. Whereas Eros is simply an agent of passion, Aphrodite is portrayed as a deliberate schemer acting directly to destroy her victims. Unlike Phaedra, Iole and Semele are victims of the passion of others (Heracles, Zeus) and the Chorus deliberately ignore other causes of their violent fates (the bad faith of Eurytus and the scheming of Hera), focusing instead on the power of passion to wreck lives. Yet all three women are portrayed as victims of violence – exploited by Aphrodite. The use of such sinister examples helps convey a sense of the foreboding of the Chorus as they await the outcome of the Nurse's scheme.

Review of the first *stasimon* (516–45)

- How do the themes of the *stasimon* reflect or develop the themes and issues of the First Episode?
- How has the Servant's warning to Hippolytus (95–104) been reiterated in the *stasimon*?
- Consider how the *stasimon* might be staged for a modern audience, unfamiliar with the myths and details of Greek religious practice.

O sacred wall of Thebes! O spring of Dirce!
You could tell how Cypris comes in stealth: 540
For she betrothed the mother of twice-born Bacchus
To the flaming thunderbolt and
Under a murderous fate laid her to sleep.
Cypris breathes disaster on all things
As she darts about like a bee.   545

Aphrodite and Eros. Red-figure lekythos (detail), c. 420–400 BC.

SECOND EPISODE (546–708)
Focus on Phaedra
At some point during the *stasimon* Phaedra has moved upstage towards the door of the *skēnē* (stage building; see Fig. B, page 123) which represents the palace. Suspense is generated as she faces an agonising wait to discover the outcome of the Nurse's scheme – yet the fact that the voices within are audible suggests the Nurse has caused an uproar.

Contrasting responses
Having detected Hippolytus' raised voice, Phaedra realises she is 'finished' (555). After a brief exclamation (550) her remaining speeches down to 576 are delivered in *iambics* (the customary metre for spoken dialogue, see 257n). In contrast, the Chorus sing in *dochmiacs* (a highly agitated lyric metre). There is a dramatically effective contrast between the dismay and shock of the Chorus and the heavy resignation of Phaedra, who already understands the full implications of what is happening within.

557 You are by the door The Chorus generally do not interfere directly in the action of Greek tragedy. Euripides here uses this convention to force Phaedra into the further agony of relaying to the Chorus the dispute between Hippolytus and the Nurse.
- What is the dramatic effect of starting the quarrel between the Nurse and Hippolytus offstage?

PHAEDRA   Women, be quiet! I am ruined.

CHORUS   What is it inside that alarms you, Phaedra?

PHAEDRA   Wait – I want to hear what those indoors are saying.

CHORUS   I will be quiet. Yet this sounds ominous.

PHAEDRA   Ah, no! No!   550
                       Misery! Oh my misfortune!

CHORUS   Why are you crying? What are you shouting?
                  Tell me, mistress, what have you heard
                  That frightens you, overpowering your mind?

PHAEDRA   I am finished. Stand by the door and listen   555
          To the uproar in the palace.

CHORUS   You are by the door – the news from inside
                          Is yours to convey.
            Tell me, tell me: what has happened that is so terrible?

PHAEDRA   It is the son of the horse-loving Amazon, Hippolytus,   560
          Who shouts. He is hurling terrible insults at my servant.

CHORUS   I hear the voice, but cannot make it out.
                   The shouting comes through the gate,
                          Reaching you clearly.

PHAEDRA   Yes, it is clear enough: he calls her a wicked matchmaker,   565
          A betrayer of her master's marriage-bed.

CHORUS   How terrible! Dear lady, you are betrayed.
                 What counsel can I give you now?
                       Your secret is out,
                       Ruin is upon you –   570
                Alas, betrayed by one dear to you.

Hippolytus' second appearance

In the Prologue Hippolytus appeared relaxed and in his element. Fresh from the hunt and accompanied by friends and attendants, he offered prayer to Artemis and confidently dismissed the warnings of the Servant. Here, however, he faces more stressful circumstances and this offers the audience a chance to examine his weaknesses.

Hippolytus' reaction

577 Mother Earth! Revealing rays of the Sun! Characters in Greek tragedy often call the elements as witnesses (see, especially, *Medea*) or address them at moments of high emotion. In Euripides' *Electra* the heroine cries out in joy to the earth and the chariot of the sun when she hears that her brother Orestes has murdered their wicked stepfather Aegisthus. Here, in contrast, Hippolytus cries out in horror, but his invocations may also be a gasp for fresh air as he is escaping the pollution (see 306n) of what the Nurse has just disclosed to him within the confines of the palace.

579–92 The *stichomythia* in these lines becomes heated (see page 28).
584 clasp your knees This is the second time the Nurse has performed the act of supplication (see page 28).

○ Using clues from lines 315–29 and 582–4, consider how to stage the Nurse's two acts of supplication: should her gestures be identical each time? How might the physical differences between Hippolytus and Phaedra affect each supplication?

Hippolytus an oath-breaker? (589)

The Nurse, no doubt aware of the danger to herself, had forced Hippolytus to swear an oath of silence before revealing Phaedra's secret (588). When she reminds him of it, he claims the oath was made by his 'tongue' but does not bind his 'heart'. This line became notorious among Euripides' contemporaries as evidence of his sophistry (see page 40) and the suspect morality in his plays, and Aristophanes referred to it at least three times – twice in *Frogs* and once in *Thesmophoriazousai*. However, it is unlikely that Hippolytus means he can go back on oaths, especially given his self-professed virtue (see **'Self-control'**, page 8). The line is perhaps better understood as an outburst, or even a claim by which Hippolytus hopes to preserve the independence of his pure heart from the stain of what he has heard.

● How might Phaedra interpret this line? How do you interpret it?

PHAEDRA   She has spoken of my misfortune and she has killed me.
  She acted kindly, but found the wrong cure for my sickness.

CHORUS   What now? What will you do in this impossible situation?

PHAEDRA   The only thing now is to die as soon as possible.   575
  That is the only remedy for the disasters I now face.

HIPPOLYTUS   Mother Earth! Revealing rays of the Sun!
  What foul, unutterable words I have heard!

NURSE   Quiet, boy, before someone hears you shouting.

HIPPOLYTUS   How can I be silent after the monstrous things   580
  I've heard?

NURSE   Please, by your arm, by your right hand, I beg you!

HIPPOLYTUS   Keep your hands away from me! Don't touch my cloak!

NURSE   Then I will clasp your knees: don't destroy me!

HIPPOLYTUS   How could I if, as you claim, you've said nothing wrong? 585

NURSE   These words, child, are not for all to hear.

HIPPOLYTUS   Surely fine words are finer when spoken in public?

NURSE   Child, do not betray the oath you swore to me.

HIPPOLYTUS   It was my tongue that swore – no oath binds my heart.

NURSE   Child, what will you do? Destroy those dear to you?   590

HIPPOLYTUS   I spit on you. No one immoral is dear to me.

NURSE   Show forgiveness. To err is human, child.

Hippolytus' condemnation of women (593–644)

The vehemence of Hippolytus' hostility towards women in this speech is striking; his quest for purity and devotion to Artemis (a female) do not automatically entail such hatred.

Staging the speech

Throughout the speech Phaedra remains on the stage. Hippolytus does not once address her directly.

Depersonalising women (593–600)

Hippolytus asks the impossible: that children could be begotten without women. This rhetorical device expresses his loathing, but also reveals two key features of his world-view: firstly, his assumption that producing offspring is the only valuable contribution a woman can make; secondly, his desire for a world free from the complications of sexual emotion. Compare Euripides' *Medea*, where Jason expresses a similar wish.

- Why do you think Hippolytus calls women a 'false currency'? What does this choice of words suggest about his value system?

601–2 A few lines in this play (601–2, 610–13, 639, 858–60, 900–1, 1018, 1039) have been dismissed as spurious by commentators. Here the reference to the bride-price paid by husbands (common in the Homeric age) conflicts with the reference to a dowry paid by the father (see 603–9n).

603 Here is proof This is very much the language of schoolboy rhetoric and seems naive in this context. The Athenian audience might think of the arrogant young men taught by the Sophists (see **'Sophistry 1'**, page 40 and 490n) to challenge traditional morality.

603–9 In fifth-century BC Athens women were at all times deemed to be under the ownership of a *kyrios* (lord). The 'dowry' aids Hippolytus' argument here as it suggests that a father is willing to pay to be free of the responsibility of ownership. The depersonalisation continues as women are described as a 'burden' and as objects to be adorned (605–8).

610–13 Hippolytus here claims that either the bride or her family are a nuisance to a husband.

- Do these lines seem to fit with the rest of the speech?

617 clever women This prejudice was widespread in Athens, where women were generally uneducated. In *Medea* the heroine complains that her reputation for cleverness precedes her. Hippolytus, however, extends his prejudice to women lacking intelligence, whom he deems 'useless' (616) and calls nonentities (614 – in Greek: *to mēden*, literally: 'the nothing').

HIPPOLYTUS   Zeus! Why did you send women – a false currency,
A curse on men – to dwell in the sunlit world?
If you wanted to sow a race of mortals, you should not   595
Have had it come from women! Instead, men could buy
The seed of children in exchange for bronze, or iron,
Or a weight of gold placed in your temples, each offering
Whatever he could afford from the value of his estate.
Then they could live in their houses free of women.   600
[Yet now if we choose to bring this evil into our homes, we
Must first pay a hefty price for the loss of our prosperity.]
Here is proof that woman is a great evil: her father, who
Has conceived and fed her, provides her with a dowry
To get her out of his house and be rid of his burden.   605
Then her husband takes the ruinous creature into his home.
He, poor wretch, takes pleasure in heaping beautiful
Accessories on his useless idol, decking her out with clothes –
Poor man, draining his house of wealth.
[He has no choice: if he marries into a good family, taking   610
Pleasure in his in-laws is the only way to preserve a union he
Finds distasteful; but if he gets a good wife with a useless family
He's hard pressed to make the good compensate for the bad.]
A nonentity would be the easiest type to marry,
But such a woman, once she'd settled in one's house,   615
With her silly ways, would be useless.
Yet I despise clever women: let no woman smarter
Than she should be ever set foot in my house. For
Cypris fosters greater mischief in clever women; at least
The brainless one lacks the wit to do anything wrong.   620

621–6 Hippolytus focuses his attack on aspects of womanhood that are more pertinent to the present situation. Although women have no role in the *polis* (city-state – the sphere of public affairs), they have servants who can traffic their schemes to the outside world. Hippolytus has wrongly assumed that the Nurse was acting under Phaedra's specific instructions.

628 my father's sacred marriage-bed
- Is it consistent of Hippolytus to describe a marriage-bed in this way?
- We learned from 588 that Hippolytus had sworn an oath of silence, but here (627–8) he seems to reveal what he had sworn to conceal. Does this count as a breaking of the oath?

629–31 running water This recalls the 'river springs' of Hippolytus' opening prayer to Artemis (72); it is to this world of purity that Hippolytus wishes to return as he feels 'polluted' (see 306n) by the very presence of Phaedra and the Nurse.

632–8 Although Hippolytus grudgingly admits he will not break the oath, his promise to return when Theseus returns constitutes a threat that would make Phaedra uneasy.

638 and your mistress
- What effect might this direct reference have on Phaedra?

643 teach them self-control *sōphrosynē* again. Hippolytus previously claimed that access to Artemis' 'untouched meadow' was denied to all but those whose self-control was 'not taught' (73–5n). While he considers women 'always wicked' (642), he does at least think they can be taught some form of self-control or good sense.
- Compare Hippolytus' idea of *sōphrosynē* here with his earlier mention of it (see page 8). Is he consistent in his views? How do his beliefs about *sōphrosynē* contrast with those of Phaedra (394, 406n) and the Nurse (483n)?

Hippolytus' speech: reflection, persuasion or self-justification?

With his 'proof' delivered, Hippolytus storms from the stage. While the speech offers a clear message, the circumstances that prompted it, not to mention Hippolytus' youth and immaturity, need due consideration.
- Do you think this speech represents a 'heat of the moment' response that Hippolytus, like the Nurse earlier, may later moderate, or does his hatred of women seem ingrained?
- What might Phaedra's physical response be to Hippolytus' tirade? How might she and the Nurse be positioned on the stage in relation to Hippolytus?

A woman should have no servant to attend her,
They should live with wild beasts, fanged and dumb;
That way they'd have no one to speak to
And no gossip with servants to swap in return.
As it is they sit indoors, scheming wicked plans   625
Which their servants pass on to the outside world.
In just such a way you have come, you evil piece of work,
To negotiate a union in my father's sacred marriage-bed.
I will rinse out my ears with running water to cleanse
Myself of your words. How could I ever commit such a sin   630
When even to *hear* this makes me feel polluted? Know this,
Woman: it is only my piety that saves you. If I'd not been
Tricked, caught off guard, made to swear the oath,
I could never have been stopped from revealing this affair to
My father. As it is, I shall keep my distance from the palace   635
And hold my tongue, as long as Theseus remains abroad.
But when my father returns then so will I, and I'll watch
To see how you – and your mistress – meet his eye.
[And after your outrageous behaviour – I'll know.]
Curse you! I can never get my fill of hating women,   640
However much I talk. I know I'm always harping on
About them, but they're always wicked.
Let someone else teach them self-control,
Or leave me to trample them down as long as I can.

INTERLUDE: Phaedra's lament (645–56)

These lines act as a response to the Chorus's lament at 358–69, in which they sympathised with Phaedra following the disclosure of her incestuous desire. Here Phaedra reciprocates by considering the pressures women often face (645–6), before contemplating her inescapable fate.

647 as I stumble Another use of the wrestling metaphor (*sphallō*, see notes on 6, 176 and 253). Here it refers to neither the schemes of the gods nor the inflexibility of principles, but to the Nurse's disastrous intervention. Yet it is worth recalling the Nurse's prayer to Cypris (513–14): ultimately it is the goddess who has tripped up Phaedra.

Speech and silence 2

A major theme throughout the play is the danger and fallibility of words. The drama is structured around issues of disclosure and concealment. As the knot metaphor (648–9) suggests, words can do irreparable damage. Phaedra must still find a way to 'unravel' the knot by hiding the catastrophe from Theseus, while much of the remainder of the play will hinge on whether Hippolytus keeps his promised silence (636).

- Consider how words have propelled the action. Have the characters succeeded in their efforts to use speech to control their circumstances and achieve their goals?

650 I have got what I deserved Again (see **'Phaedra's view of human nature'**, page 34), Phaedra believes she is culpable for her feelings.

659 Most treacherous The Greek word (*pankakistē*) means 'utterly bad in every way' – contrast Phaedra's more lenient judgement (572–3).

660 Zeus, my grandfather Phaedra's father, Minos (see page v), was a son of Zeus and Europa.

662 Did I not tell you
- Look again at lines 480–515. How accurate is the version of that conversation given by Phaedra in 662–5?
- What is motivating Phaedra to launch such a stinging attack on the Nurse in these lines (659–65)?

666–7 he ... Will denounce me to his father As at 347, Phaedra finds it difficult to utter Hippolytus' name. She has no reason to believe that Hippolytus will keep silent.
- Do you think Phaedra's intention to 'think again' (665) is motivated by hostility to Hippolytus or by the desire to preserve her own reputation?

668 aged Pittheus Hippolytus' mentor (see 11n).

PHAEDRA   Unhappy, ill-starred   645
                         Is a woman's fate!
               Now, as I stumble, what way, what words
                   Can I find to unravel the knot
                     These words have tied?
                    I have got what I deserved.   650
            O Earth! O Light! How shall I escape my fate?
               How, friends, can I conceal my grief?
           What god, what mortal, will appear beside me
               To counsel or assist me in my wrongdoing?
      For my suffering is moving inexorably to the edge of life.   655
               I am the most unfortunate of women.

CHORUS   Alas! It is finished. Your servant's craft, mistress,
    Has failed and all is lost.

PHAEDRA   Most treacherous of women, wrecker of friends,
    See what you have done to me! May Zeus, my grandfather,   660
    Blast you with fire, destroy you root and branch!
    Did I not foresee your purpose? Did I not tell you to keep
    Quiet about the very things that now bring shame on me?
    But you could not contain yourself, and so no longer will
    I die with my reputation intact. Now I need to think again.   665
    For *he*, his anger whetted,
    Will denounce me to his father for your crimes,
    Will tell the aged Pittheus of my troubles
    And fill the whole land with the scandal.
    May you die – you and anyone else who's quick   670
    To help their friends by wicked means, against their will.

The Nurse's defence (672–9)

The Nurse accepts her 'wrongdoing' but on practical rather than moral grounds – because the *outcome* of her efforts was negative. True to her beliefs (uncertainty about what exists beyond the grave, see 188–90, and her general view that pleasure is preferable to adherence to rigid principles, see 252–6, 425–70), she believes the end justifies the means, and that 'success' (the Greek word *tuchai* suggests 'luck' as well as 'success') governs human affairs.

- 'I wish I hadn't / Found what I did' (676–7) How far do you think the Nurse's blunders are a result of a genuine failure to comprehend the moral positions of Hippolytus and Phaedra?
- What might the Nurse have in mind when she says 'you can be saved' (683)?
- How might the Nurse see to her own 'affairs' (687)?
- The Nurse does not speak again in the play. At what point would you have her leave the stage? Would she be reluctant to leave?

Speech and silence 3

Phaedra learns, all too late, the danger of speech, as her abrupt order to the Nurse, 'Stop talking!' (684), demonstrates.

The oath of the Chorus (688–91)

Phaedra intends to die (700) and is already making provisions to preserve her reputation after death. She asks the Chorus, as witnesses both of the preceding action and of what is to follow, to guarantee their silence.

694 give my sons a reputable life Phaedra's preoccupation with her reputation (see page 34) may seem selfish at times, but she also shows concern for her sons (see also 303), her own family, the 'royal house of Crete' (696, see also 331–8) and Theseus himself.

Dark hints (696–8)

Already (693–4) Phaedra has hinted that there may be more to her death than simple suicide.

- Explore the ambiguities of the phrase 'For the sake of a single life' (698). Is Phaedra simply referring to herself?

701 You must not talk like that! The Greek literally means 'keep to words of good omen'; the Chorus fear that mention of suicide might incur divine displeasure. In 702 Phaedra overrides the advice, proving that her resolve is unshakeable.

NURSE Mistress, I can see why you blame my wrongdoing;
  Shock overpowers your judgement,
  But I can answer the charge if you will listen.
  I brought you up and I am devoted to you.   675
  In seeking to cure your sickness I wish I hadn't
  Found what I did. But if I had succeeded,
  I would have been considered wise.
  A reputation for wit depends on success.
PHAEDRA Is that fair? Do I deserve this?   680
  That you wound me and then try to make it up?
NURSE Too much talk. I went too far,
  But even now you can be saved, child.
PHAEDRA Stop talking! You gave me bad advice before
  And what you tried to do was wrong.   685
  Get out of my way and give some thought
  To your affairs – it is for me to set my own in order.
  And you, noble daughters of Trozen, grant me this request:
  Keep silent about what you have heard here.
CHORUS I swear by holy Artemis, daughter of Zeus,   690
  Never to reveal your troubles.
PHAEDRA Thank you. I will say one thing more:
  I have found a way out of my misery,
  A way to give my sons a reputable life
  And do myself good, even as things have turned out.   695
  For I will never shame the royal house of Crete,
  Or face Theseus in this atmosphere of shame,
  For the sake of a single life.
CHORUS What do you intend to do? Some irreparable harm?
PHAEDRA To die. As for how, that is something I must decide.   700
CHORUS You must not talk like that!
PHAEDRA And you must give me good advice.

703 Cypris, my destroyer When the Nurse turned to the statue of Aphrodite (513–14), she proved instrumental in moving Aphrodite's plan forward. Here Phaedra, conscious that her actions will 'delight' the goddess, seems to echo her servant's role.

703–8 In Phaedra's final speech a further sinister note is added as she claims disaster will strike 'this very day', echoing the words of Aphrodite in the Prologue (54). Her intention to involve Hippolytus in some way is made explicit (705–8), suggesting that she has been genuinely hurt by the 'contempt' he showed her previously.

Sōphrosynē 2: teaching self-control (708)

Phaedra, perhaps spurred by Hippolytus' earlier dismissive comment (643n), intends to educate her stepson as to the true nature of 'self-control'. Whereas Hippolytus thinks of *sōphrosynē* as an innate quality that keeps its possessor pure (see page 8), for Phaedra it is a social virtue, closely related to the concept of *aidōs* (see 378–83 and note) and therefore involving restraint – notably in one's dealings with others (see 394, 406n and 483n).

- This translation has attempted to render *sōphrosynē* consistently as 'self-control'. Do you think any of the following possible translations works better: *prudence, discretion, moderation, sobriety, temperance, chastity, soundness of mind*?

Review of the Second Episode

This scene presents a very different side of Hippolytus' character, as well as showing Phaedra's resourcefulness in overcoming her frailty.

- Consider the dramatic effect of Phaedra's final burst of energy in condemning the Nurse and planning her own death: does the scene focus more sympathy on Phaedra?
- To what extent have the weaknesses of the human characters contributed to the furtherance of Aphrodite's plan (see **'Review: the character and plan of Aphrodite'**, page 6)?

I will delight Cypris, my destroyer, when I end
My life this very day, victim of a bitter love.
Yet in dying I will bring another down, so that   705
He may learn not to treat my suffering with contempt.
By sharing in this affliction of mine,
He will learn what self-control is.

Phaedra and Hippolytus *by Pierre-Narcisse Guérin, 1802. This painting,
based on Racine's* Phèdre, *depicts Hippolytus' rejection of a humiliated
Phaedra, Theseus' anger towards his son, and a conspiratorial Nurse (far
right).*

SECOND *STASIMON* (709–46)

In the first strophic pair (709–28) the Chorus long to fly far away from the difficulties in Trozen. In the second strophic pair (729–46) they lament Phaedra's ill fortune and envision her impending suicide.

714 Adriatic coast The Adriatic Sea, more specifically the Gulf of Venice, which the Greeks called Adrias.

715 Eridanus A mythical river later identified with the river Po in northern Italy.

Phaethon (716–18)

Phaethon, son of Helios the sun god, lost control of his father's chariot and nearly destroyed the earth (an event vividly portrayed in Ovid's *Metamorphoses*). This disaster struck Phaethon after he was shocked by his mother's revelation that Helios was his real father. It is no coincidence that the story of an innocent young man who faced disaster should occur to the Chorus: in this *stasimon* their wish to escape is combined with a growing concern for another 'innocent' young man: Hippolytus.

717 piteous sisters Known as the Heliads, they lamented their brother's death and were turned into poplar trees. Their tears became 'amber'.

721 Hesperides The nymphs who guarded golden apples in a western land at the edge of the world, near the mountains of 'Atlas', a Titan who held up the rim of the sky and is said to have been turned to stone by the Gorgon's head (the 'hallowed boundary of heaven / Which Atlas keeps' (724–5) is modern-day Gibraltar).

Longing for the impossible

A recurring motif in the play is the wish for the unattainable: Phaedra ached to join the hunt (200–24), while Hippolytus wanted a world without women (593–600). Here the Chorus long for the fabled land where Zeus married Hera; yet the 'sea-lord' (Poseidon) denies mortals access (722). The Chorus's wish expresses discontent with the human condition, and the suggestion is that true 'happiness' is reserved only for the gods (728).

729 O white-winged Cretan ship In the second strophic pair (729–46) the Chorus reflect on a rather different journey. The white sails of Phaedra's ship recall the story of the death of Theseus' father, Aegeus, whose instruction to his son (that in the event of his death in Crete his crew should hoist a black sail on the return journey) was tragically forgotten (see page v).

732 The Chorus capture the bitter-sweet tone of Phaedra's thwarted hopes and doomed adventure with the oxymoronic (seemingly contradictory, from the Greek for 'sharp-blunt') phrase 'bliss of an ill-fated marriage'.

CHORUS   I wish I could hide, high up,
          Beneath crags,   710
    Where a god could give me wings to fly
       As a bird among the flocks.
        I wish I could be lifted
   Over the sea wave of the Adriatic coast,
      Over the waters of Eridanus,   715
      Into whose dark waves, in grief,
      Phaethon's piteous sisters pour
  The amber-gleaming radiance of their tears.

    Then I could find my journey's end
       Among the apple groves,   720
  Upon the shore of the singing Hesperides;
   Where the sea-lord of the dark shallows
     Gives sailors passage no more,
But marks instead the hallowed boundary of heaven
        Which Atlas keeps.   725
 Here by Zeus' marriage-bed flow blissful streams,
  Here holy Earth, with her abundant gifts,
   Augments the happiness of the gods.

    O white-winged Cretan ship,
    Over the brine-pounding wave   730
You brought my queen from her prosperous home
To win her the bliss of an ill-fated marriage.

Imagery of foreboding (733–46)

The second strophic pair (729–46) reverses the motif of escape, bringing our attention back to the imminent death of Phaedra. The 'wings to fly' (711) become the 'bird of ill omen' (733) that is Phaedra. Her journey is from the legends of her birthplace, Crete ('Minos' land', 734), to Athens ('Mounichus' is another mythical Athenian king), where she fell in love with Hippolytus, and on to the catastrophe of her hanging, which the Chorus seem to visualise (741–3). Phaedra's 'white neck' (743) echoes the 'white' sails (729), an ironic parallel between the beginning and end of her journey. The 'twisted rope-ends' (736) of the fateful boat are echoed by the 'noose' (742), which also recalls the imagery of the 'knot / These words have tied' (648–9; see **'Speech and silence 2'**, page 58).

Review of the second *stasimon*

745 the glory of a good name The Chorus imagine that Phaedra can cancel the shame of her desire for Hippolytus through suicide.

- How is a contrast in mood between the two strophic pairs created? How might this contrast illuminate the crucial differences between gods and men?
- How has the second *stasimon* altered your impression of Phaedra?
- O How does the mood of this *stasimon* differ from that of the first (516–45) and how might you reflect this difference if you were choreographing both?

THIRD EPISODE (747–1092)

The visualisation of the Chorus (741–3) is immediately proven accurate, as a 'voice within' the palace is heard, urgently calling for help. The original manuscripts give these lines to either a *therapaina* (lady-in-waiting) or a *trophos* (the Greek word used to signify the Nurse).

- O How might it be more dramatically effective to have the lines within spoken by the Nurse?

The Chorus inert (749–60)

Despite the urgency of the voice from within, the Chorus fail to act. They consider the queen already dead and dither when called upon to help cut the noose, claiming there is no point, that young male attendants are better qualified to help, and lastly – no doubt influenced by the disastrous results of the Nurse's meddling – that 'it is risky to interfere' (756).

- Is the Chorus's failure to act a betrayal of Phaedra? Having shared in her deliberations, what attitude might they have towards her death?

Twice a bird of ill omen,
Once as she flew from Minos' land to glorious Athens,
And again at Mounichus' shores   735
When they bound fast the twisted rope-ends
And set foot on the mainland.

And so her soul was crippled by an unholy passion,
Aphrodite's cruel sickness broke her spirit;
And now, overwhelmed by hard misfortune,   740
From the beams of the bridal chamber
She will fasten a noose and hang herself,
Fixing it round her white neck,
Ashamed of her ugly fate,
Choosing instead the glory of a good name   745
By freeing her heart of its painful desire.

VOICE WITHIN   Help! You, near the palace, anyone, bring help
Quickly! Our mistress, Theseus' wife, is trapped in a noose!
CHORUS   Alas. It is over. The queen is no more,
She has strangled herself and is hanging by a rope.   750
VOICE   Hurry! Someone bring a two-edged sword
To cut the rope around her neck.
CHORUS   What shall we do, friends? Should we enter the palace
To free the queen from the noose she has tied?
But why? Are there no young men to attend her?   755
In life it is risky to interfere.
VOICE   Set her poor body straight, lay out her limbs.
This will be a bitter homecoming for my master.
CHORUS   It sounds like she's dead, poor woman –
If they are now laying out her corpse.   760

Theseus: first impressions

Theseus, the king of Trozen and Athens, enters, wearing a garland that signifies a successful answer from the Delphic Oracle, which he has just visited (see 271n). It is not unheard of for a major character to appear for the first time so late in a Greek tragedy. In Sophocles' *Trachiniae*, a play written at about the same time as *Hippolytus*, Heracles appears after almost a thousand lines.

In both plays a great deal of suspense is created by the delayed appearance of the most immediately recognisable character. Theseus, like Heracles, is a universally renowned hero, a retired man of action, yet previous references to him in this play have been largely negative. He was required to purify himself after slaying his cousins, the Pallantides (33), and in the *parodos* the Chorus refer to his reputation for infidelity; while Phaedra's reference to Ariadne (333) recalls the famous tradition that he abandoned her after she helped him escape the labyrinth (see page v; see also **'Theseus the womaniser'**, page 18).

762–3 Does my house not ... welcome Theseus' first instinct is to complain that his return from consulting an oracle has not been properly acknowledged. When he discovers the truth, he describes himself as 'a pilgrim of misfortune' (778), while in contrast the Chorus, in their short lament, devote their thoughts entirely to the dead queen (781–7).

765 the aged Pittheus (see 11n) It is quite appropriate that Theseus should assume the eldest person in the palace had died.

● What impression of Theseus do you get from his opening speech?

775 That is all we know The Chorus lie to keep their oath of silence (see **'The oath of the Chorus'**, page 60).

Ekkyklēma

Greek theatre made use of some special effects, in particular the wheeled platform (*ekkyklēma*) used to depict tableaux – most commonly (as here, in Aeschylus' *Agamemnon* and Sophocles' *Electra*) of corpses. The *ekkyklēma* may have revolved, which would have focused the audience's attention onto the precise moment of revelation. This would no doubt have added to the drama here and raised the intensity of Theseus' response.

THESEUS   Women, what is all this noise inside about? Why can
I hear the servants shouting? Does my house not see fit
To open its gates and give me the warm welcome a pious
Traveller should expect? I hope nothing has happened
To the aged Pittheus? He is well advanced in years,   765
But it would grieve me if he were to leave this house.

CHORUS   The misfortune you face does not concern the old, Theseus.
It is the young whose death brings you grief.

THESEUS   What? Have my children lost their lives?

CHORUS   No, they are alive, but their mother's death   770
Will bring you terrible pain.

THESEUS   What? My wife dead? How did this happen?

CHORUS   She fixed a noose and hanged herself.

THESEUS   Numbed by grief, or was it some other misfortune?

CHORUS   That is all we know. I too have only just come here,   775
Theseus, to lament for your woes.

THESEUS   Alas! Why is my head crowned with this garland
Of leaves, a pilgrim of misfortune?
Servants, undo the locks, unbar the gates, so I can see
The bitter sight of my wife, whose death has ruined me.   780

CHORUS   Unhappy woman in your wretched misery!
                    By your suffering, by your actions
                    You have destroyed this house.
                          So bold a step:
                    Violent death by unholy means,   785
                    A fall inflicted by your own hand.
              Poor woman, what darkened your life so?

Theseus' lament (788–834)

The revelation of Phaedra's corpse (see '*Ekkyklēma*', page 68) is a moment of high drama, and Theseus' lament sustains the intensity. Euripides alternates between an emotional lyric metre (*dochmiacs*) and the more reflective metre of spoken verse (*iambics* – 792–3, 798–9, 803–4, 817–18, 822–3, 827–8).

- How does the alternation of metre illuminate the struggle Theseus faces in comprehending what has happened?
- Contrast this use of different metres with the earlier use in the scene between Phaedra and the Chorus (546–71; see also '**Contrasting responses**', page 50).

The captive bride

Theseus' imagery of an 'ocean of troubles' (797) and his depiction of Phaedra as an escaped 'bird' (803) recall the Chorus's description of her fateful voyage from Crete (see 733 and '**Imagery of foreboding**', page 66) and serve as reminders of Phaedra's status: she was brought from Crete as a captive (see page v). In Seneca's *Phaedra* this status is made clearer when Phaedra describes herself as 'a hostage bound to a hostile house' (90, trans. Watling).

804 Hades The king of the underworld, brother of Zeus and Poseidon. Here, by the figure of speech called *metonymy*, his name is used to stand for the underworld itself.

810 the sins of an ancestor Theseus suspects that some 'pollution' (792; see 33n, 306n) or curse inherited from a remote ancestor has brought about the current disaster. If, as seems likely, his consultation of an oracle was in atonement for his killing of his cousins (the Pallantides, see 33n),
he must now be questioning the successful answer he received (see '**Theseus: first impressions**', page 68).

- Compare Theseus' attempt to explain his misfortune (792, 810) with Phaedra's similar attempt to explain hers (331–6). Which attempt evokes more *pathos*?

THESEUS
O my afflictions!
Ah, I have suffered
The worst of my trials.   790
O misfortune,

A pollution unforeseen, sent by some avenger,
How you crush me and all my household!

This destruction makes
Life unbearable;   795
In misery I face
An ocean of troubles

So vast that I can never swim free of it,
Never breast the waves of this disaster.

What words, poor wife, can I find?   800
How can I discover the truth
Behind your ill-starred fate?

Like a bird you have vanished from my hands,
And with a headlong leap dashed down to Hades.

O the pain of suffering!   805
How piteous is this pain!
From somewhere long ago
I must have incurred
Misfortune from the gods
For the sins of an ancestor.   810

811–12 These lines seem unsympathetic or dispassionate. It was common for choruses in Greek tragedy to console the bereaved by making the point that others have also suffered such a terrible loss. The Chorus in Euripides' *Alcestis* make the same point to Admetus on the loss of his wife.

817 precious company It was unusual for husbands to seek *homilia* ('company') from their wives regularly; in a fifth-century BC Athenian house there were separate men's and women's quarters.

Theseus fighting the Minotaur. Attic black-figured amphora (detail), sixth century BC.

822–3 For the first time in thirty lines, Theseus addresses the servants who brought in Phaedra's body (see 779).
- How might the presence of servants increase the dramatic impact of the scene?
- How might the servants be arranged on stage? Would they remain close to the corpse and the wheeled platform, or stand at a respectful distance?

Review of Theseus' lament (788–834)
- How personal do you find the lines that describe Phaedra or are addressed directly to her?
- Consider Theseus' evaluation of his loss in these lines: what impact does Phaedra's death seem to have on him?
- What does Theseus' lament reveal about his character?

CHORUS   You are not alone in suffering this, lord: you have
Lost a cherished wife, but so have many others.

THESEUS   In my misery
                              I long for dusk
                              Beneath the earth,   815
                       In death to live in darkness.
                 I have lost your most precious company,
          It is not only your own death you have brought about.

                              Poor wife,
                    Let me hear from someone how   820
                   The thought of death entered your heart.
              Who can tell me what has happened here? Do I keep
            A servant rabble in the royal house for nothing?

                      Ah! What I feel – for you:
                    Grief, I have seen so much pain   825
                          Befall this house,
                 Unbearable, unutterable. I am ruined:
              My house deserted, my children orphaned.

                      Ah! You have deserted me,
                      Deserted me, dear wife,   830
                       The best of all women
                        The light of the sun,
                       Or star-filled brilliance
                          Of night has seen.

The writing tablet (835–51)

At 693–5 Phaedra warned that she had found a way to preserve her honour and throughout the ensuing lament the tension has been sustained as we wait to discover the details of her plan. The Chorus previously limited themselves to consoling Theseus and lamenting Phaedra, but upon the discovery of the *deltos* – 'writing tablet' (842) – they offer a first hint of the 'disaster to come' (840). Theseus' ignorance of its contents is poignant and adds further suspense.

- What do lines 841–51 reveal about Theseus' view of Phaedra (see 817n and **'Review of Theseus' lament'**, page 72)?
- How do lines 844–7 cast a new light on the Nurse's warning about Phaedra's sons (291–3)?
- Given Theseus' track record (see page v), how convincing do you find his reassurance at 846–7?

848 golden ring While Theseus' recognition of Phaedra's seal allows him a moment of tender recollection, the description of the ring also serves to confirm the author of the tablet's contents. The account of the painstaking process of opening the tablet again heightens suspense.

The Chorus agitated (852–60)

While Theseus reads the tablet, the Chorus await revelation of a 'fresh calamity', again in agitated *dochmiacs* (see **'Contrasting responses'**, page 50 and **'Theseus' lament'**, page 70). Since the Chorus's sense of foreboding might attract suspicion and jeopardise their oath to Phaedra (688–91), it should be assumed that Theseus cannot hear these lines.

858–60 Although the phrase 'bring … to the ground' recalls the wrestling motif found elsewhere in the play with the use of the verb *sphallō* (6n, 176n, 647n), these lines are considered spurious because the Chorus merely speculate about a 'fearful omen', whereas before they seemed certain that the tablet would reveal something terrible (852–3).

| CHORUS | Unhappy man, | 835 |

Such evil within your house!
My eyes well up,
And shed tears at your misfortune –
Yet I have long been trembling
At the disaster to come. 840

THESEUS   But look at this:
A writing tablet hanging from her dear hand?
Does it want to tell me fresh news?
Did the poor woman write a letter begging me
To respect our marriage and our children? 845
Courage, poor wife: no other woman shall ever enter
Theseus' marriage-bed or house.
And see, the imprint of her golden ring, a smiling sign
To me from my wife, who is no more.
Come, let me untie the cord that fastens the seal 850
And see what the tablet wants to tell me.

CHORUS   Ah! This is a fresh calamity
The god inflicts, to follow on the last.
What can I hope for but death
After what has happened? 855
Alas! The house of my king
Is ruined; it is no more!
[God, hear me if you can, I pray: do not bring
This house to the ground. For like a seer I dread
A fearful omen coming on its way.] 860

Theseus' second lament (864–70, 872–5)

Once Theseus has absorbed what he has read, he breaks into a further lament. The greater violence of his emotion is conveyed by the use of a variety of lyric metres.

○ How might you convey the different reactions of those on stage (Theseus, male servants and female attendants) to Phaedra's death and to the contents of the tablet?

Speech and silence 4

This motif (see pages 34, 58, 60) is made all the more acute by the fact that Phaedra's silence in death is broken by the tablet which 'screams out horrors' (864).

875 Hear me, citizens The Greek phrase *iō polis* acts almost as a formal summons as Theseus invites the community to bear witness to the crime committed against him. The rest of the scene takes on the characteristics of a trial, with the defendant initially indicted in his absence.

○ How might you stage the citizens' response to this line? Would Theseus address the audience? Would the Chorus react differently from the others?

877 the sacred eye of Zeus Zeus is the guardian of the moral law among men, and nothing that mortals do escapes his eye. Like the sun, which is invoked later in Hippolytus' speech of defence (980), the eye of Zeus is a universal witness.

878–80 The successful conclusion of Aphrodite's plan moves significantly closer, and as if to emphasise the point Aphrodite's words are echoed in the phrase 'this very day' (see 54, 703–8n). At such moments, human characters appear little more than instruments of divine will. Theseus, however, is unsure if the three curses bequeathed to him by 'Father Poseidon' will work (see 42–3).

Judge and jury

Phaedra's testimony is taken as incontrovertible proof of guilt and before Hippolytus can even defend himself, he has been cursed (878–80) and, in case the curse fails, exiled (883–4). The democratic Athenian audience would immediately see a problem: Theseus is simultaneously *dikastēs* (juror), *archōn* (magistrate) and, indeed, *martys* (witness). When he talks of Hippolytus being 'struck' by exile or death, he uses the verb *plēssein* which is normally used to describe the effect of Zeus' thunderbolts.

THESEUS	Oh! This is a second horror to add to my woes.
	Unendurable, unspeakable! I am utterly ruined.
CHORUS	What is it? Tell me, if you can share it with me.
THESEUS	The tablet screams, screams out horrors.

$$\text{Where can I escape} \qquad 865$$
$$\text{The weight of these troubles?}$$
$$\text{I am ruined, destroyed.}$$
$$\text{Such a song, such a song}$$
$$\text{Have I seen in my grief}$$
$$\text{Crying out from this writing!} \qquad 870$$

CHORUS   Alas! Your words reveal the coming of new sorrows.

THESEUS

I will no longer hold this back
Locked in my mouth,
This inexorable, terrible grief.
Hear me, citizens: 875

Hippolytus has dared lay violent hands upon my wife,
Dishonouring the sacred eye of Zeus.
Father Poseidon, use one of the three curses you promised me:
Destroy my son; let him not survive this very day,
If the curses which you granted me are true.   880

CHORUS   Master, by the gods, take back the words you've uttered.
In time you will recognise your mistake. Trust me.

THESEUS   Impossible. And what is more, I will drive him
From this land; he shall be struck by one of two fates:
Either Poseidon will respect my curses and send him   885
To the house of Hades, or he will drag out a life of pain,
A wandering exile on foreign soil.

Hippolytus' third appearance

Hippolytus enters, accompanied by followers (see 1089). Very little time has passed since his tirade against women persuaded Phaedra to take action against him (see 666–9).

- From his first speech, what impression do you get of Hippolytus' relationship with his father?
- How genuine do you think Hippolytus' surprise is when he first sets eyes on Phaedra's corpse (894–7)?

Staging the scene

At this point in the play there are three groups of onlookers on stage: the Chorus, Theseus' attendants, and now also Hippolytus' followers.

○ How might the three groups be arranged on the *orchēstra* (see page 123) to illustrate their different sympathies?

899 Misfortune is no time for silence! In light of earlier reflections on speech and silence (see pages 34, 58, 60, 76), this line perhaps appears ironic when contrasted with Phaedra's order to the Nurse (684) and her conviction that silence was the best response to her passion (389–92).

Illegitimacy

Beyond the legal matter of inheritance, illegitimacy (Greek word *notheia*) to the ancient Greeks implied a lack of moral worth. Hippolytus' high moral values and education by Pittheus (see 11n) are clearly directed at countering this slur. We expect him to say that it is worse to hide the truth from *family* than from 'friends' (902–3), but his use of the vague and awkward phrase 'closer than friends' (903) shows acute awareness of his questionable status.

Sophistry 2 (904–12)

Theseus questions the value of human progress (compare the famous *stasimon* in Sophocles' *Antigone*) if people are not taught 'right thinking'. Hippolytus' response reinforces his belief that such virtue cannot be taught, and for 'teacher' he uses the word *sophistēs*, which recalls the controversial Sophists (see **'Self-control'**, page 8, and **'Sophistry 1'**, page 40). This exchange is, however, more personal than it seems. By his use of a verb ('track down') specific to one of Hippolytus' principal activities, Theseus is aiming his criticism at his son, while Hippolytus' suggestion that 'this crisis has upset your speech' (912) suggests that he views his father's words and reasoning as incoherent.

CHORUS   Here is your son Hippolytus – and just in time.
   Give up your dangerous anger, lord Theseus;
   Consider what is best for your household.   890

HIPPOLYTUS   I heard your cry, father, and have come
   With all haste. But I don't know what has made you
   Call out. Please tell me. But what is this?
   I see your wife, father – dead! This is astonishing:
   I only just left her; hardly a moment   895
   Has passed since she saw the light of day.
   What happened to her? How did she die?
   Father, I want to hear it from you.
   You are silent? Misfortune is no time for silence!
   [Even in misfortunes the heart that yearns   900
   To hear everything is found to be greedy.]
   It is surely wrong to hide your troubles from your friends,
   Let alone from those, father, who are closer than friends.

THESEUS   O, mankind, how misguided, how futile you are!
   Why is it you teach countless skills,   905
   Contrive schemes, make discoveries in every field,
   Yet one thing you fail to understand, to track down:
   How to teach right thinking to those who have no sense.

HIPPOLYTUS   The teacher you refer to would be
   A genius if he could force good sense on those who lack it. 910
   Yet this is not the time for subtle talk, father –
   I fear this crisis has upset your speech.

Two voices (913–20)

An underlying theme in the play is that aspirations are undermined by the gods and by misunderstandings and emotional conflict. Theseus' desire for transparency in judging true friends echoes Hippolytus' wish for a simpler way to acquire offspring (see **'Depersonalising women'**, page 54).

- What does Theseus' 'impossible wish' reveal about both his character and his view of Hippolytus?

Theseus' third soliloquy (925–30)

Theseus has ignored Hippolytus since he entered (891), reflecting instead on human deceit in a series of three soliloquies. Having contemplated wrong thinking (904–8) and dishonesty (913–20), here he considers the worst 'extremes' of behaviour. The direct confrontation between father and son is thus dramatically delayed, and although Hippolytus realises that he has occasioned his father's words (921–2), he has no idea how.

- What emotions do Theseus' three soliloquies (904–8, 913–20, 925–30) suggest he feels towards his son?

Hippolytus on trial

The remainder of the Third Episode (931–1092) takes the form of an *agōn* (see page 42) between father and son. Theseus' certainty at the outset is formidable, and his prosecution speech is striking to a modern reader because it is based not on forensic evidence (indeed, Hippolytus learns nothing more than the claim that he has 'dishonoured' Theseus' 'bed' – 931–2), but on an indictment of the defendant's character.

934 infected by your presence In another echo of Hippolytus' own words (see 629–31n) Theseus suggests it is pollution (*miasma*, see 306n) even to set eyes on his son.

935 look your father in the eye This is the first time Theseus has addressed Hippolytus directly (compare Hippolytus' own treatment of Phaedra, 638n). Upon learning the charge (931–3), Hippolytus had covered his face in shame, a gesture which recalls Euripides' earlier version of the story, the *Hippolytus Kalyptomenos* (*Hippolytus Veiled* – see page vi), when a more brazen Phaedra propositioned him directly. A similar confrontation occurs in Seneca's *Phaedra*, although the Phaedra in that play bears more similarity to the character in this play.

937 The man of self-control Theseus claims his son's 'self-control' is a facade. This is especially damaging to Hippolytus' version of *sōphrosynē* (for notes on *sōphrosynē* see pages 8 and 62, and 643n).

THESEUS   Ah, men should have some clear sign agreed
For friends, by which to judge their characters,
To separate the true from the false.   915
Each man should have two voices: an honest one
And the one he has already. That way,
When the wrong harboured dishonest thoughts,
The honest voice would correct it,
And we would avoid deception.   920
HIPPOLYTUS   Has some friend filled your ear with slander
Against me? Am I condemned, though guilty of nothing?
I am amazed. Your words are so insane
They amaze me, scare me out of my wits.
THESEUS   Alas. To what extremes will the mind of man go?   925
Is there any limit to its insolence, its wrongdoing?
If it grows bolder in the course of each man's life,
And each villain's wickedness exceeds the last,
The gods will be forced to add new land to the earth,
To accommodate the unjust and the wicked.   930
Look at this man: my own son, he has dishonoured
My bed and, by the evidence of this dead woman,
He is proved beyond doubt the wickedest of men.
Come, since I am already infected by your presence,
Show your face, look your father in the eye.   935
So, you are the exceptional man who communes with gods?
The man of self-control, untouched by sin – that's you, is it?
Well I would not let your boasts persuade me
To make the mistake of thinking the gods so stupid.

Orphism (940–3)

Orpheus was a legendary singer famous for his failed attempt to rescue his wife Eurydice from the underworld. The cult of Orphism, considered unorthodox in fifth-century BC Athens, viewed the soul as immortal and practised purifying rituals such as vegetarianism. By 'scribblings' Theseus means the sacred poems attributed to Orpheus. There is no evidence of an Orphic 'wild dance' and Theseus may have in mind the rituals of Bacchism (see **'Semele'**, page 48), which Hippolytus would no doubt abhor. Though Hippolytus was an initiate in the Eleusinian Mysteries (25n), his enthusiasm for the feast after the hunt (106) suggests he is not vegetarian.

- Do you think the reference to Orphism is a gibe, or might it reflect Theseus' ignorance about his son?

944–5 pursue you / With their pious words Theseus again makes pointed reference to Hippolytus' favourite pastime (see 907). The negative use of the word 'pious' (*semnos* – see 90n) recalls an inherent danger in Hippolytus' way of life: the ideal of purity, if pursued in an ostentatious way (see 940), will tend to attract charges of arrogance and hypocrisy.

- Do you think Hippolytus has been guilty of 'parading' his ideals?

946–58 After indicting Hippolytus' character, Theseus anticipates three lines of defence. The verb translated 'convicts you' (948) was the Athenian legal term for a sentencing, yet it was statutory for defendants to make 'oaths' (948) before the jury, calling the gods as witness to their innocence. Theseus implies he will not even listen to such protestations, though it might be considered his duty to do so (see **'Judge and jury'**, page 76).

- Would you expect Hippolytus to use any such lines of defence?
- How convincing do you find Theseus' arguments against them?

Theseus the hero (961–8)

Theseus' language gives a clear picture of his image of himself as a just and divinely sanctioned ruler ('god-built Athens') who governs by the 'spear'. He reinforces this by referring to his conquest of famous wrongdoers: 'Sinis of the Isthmus' at Corinth tied people to pine trees and shot them into the air to their death, while Sciron kicked his victims over a cliff when they bent down to wash his feet.

Review of Theseus' speech (925–68)

- Theseus calls Phaedra's body a 'reliable witness' (960). Do you think his assumptions are understandable in the circumstances?
- 'Like father, like son': despite their conflicting beliefs, how similar are Theseus and Hippolytus in temperament?

You may be haughty now, parade your vegetarian diet,   940
Join the wild dance with Orpheus as your lord,
Honour the inanity of his countless scribblings –
But you've been caught out! My advice to anyone is
To avoid such men as these. For while they pursue you
With their pious words, they're forming wicked plots.   945
My wife is dead: do you think that will save you?
On the contrary, you wicked man; this above all else
Convicts you. What oaths, what words spoken
To acquit you of the guilt could carry greater weight
Than this woman here? Will you claim she hated you,   950
That the bastard is the natural enemy of the true born?
You would be calling her a poor bargainer for her own life
If she gave up, out of spite for you, what was dearest to her.
Then perhaps you'll claim that men aren't subject to lust,
While women have it in their nature? I know myself   955
That when Cypris stirs a youthful heart
Young men are no more immune than women;
Though being men they have an advantage. So now –
But why should *I* challenge your words when this corpse
Before us serves as a most reliable witness?   960
Leave this country with all speed; you are an exile,
Forbidden to set foot in god-built Athens,
Or to cross the border of any land governed by my spear.
For if I give in after what I've suffered from you,
Sinis of the Isthmus will swear I never killed him,   965
But claim instead I am an idle boaster,
And Sciron's rocks beside the sea will deny
The heavy treatment I give out to criminals.
CHORUS   I do not know how to call any mortal
Fortunate; even the mightiest are overthrown.   970

Hippolytus' defence (971–1024)

Hippolytus' defence is carefully structured. After a preamble, he affirms his good character (980–94) and refutes motives that might be ascribed to him (995–1007). In between two attempts to hint at what he knows but cannot say, he swears an oath protesting his innocence (1013–20).

972–3 though fine sounding … Is anything but fine Hippolytus describes Theseus' *words* as fine sounding (*kalous* – see **'Sophistry 1'**, page 40) but regards his case as *ou* (not) *kalon*, showing that, despite wanting to appear honest, he is comfortable handling subtle ambiguities of language.

Hippolytus' plea of inexperience (974–7)

The Athenian audience, many of whom would have served as jurors, were familiar with the plea of inexperience: with no defence lawyers available, the accused had to plead their cases unassisted. Hippolytus gives a reminder of his aristocratic lifestyle; he has no experience of addressing a 'mob' (*ochlos*, see 205n), preferring to speak among 'experts'.

- How might this plea affect the attitude of the onlookers (see **'Staging the scene'**, page 78) towards Hippolytus?

Sōphrosynē 3 (981–8)

Hippolytus seeks to answer his father's charge (see 937n), but the description of the man of 'self-control' in these lines seems more like the social, civic virtue of 'good sense' than Hippolytus' earlier talk of it as a spiritual virtue of purity and abstinence (see **'Sophrosyne 1'**, and **'Self-control'**, page 8).

- How readily do you accept Hippolytus' claim to 'know how to revere the gods' (983)?
- How does his description of the bad friend (984–7) recall his impressions of Phaedra and the Nurse (621–6)?

991–2 heard / And seen in pictures Presumably in conversation with his companions and from crude vase-paintings.

- If Hippolytus' self-control is innate, does this suggest it is easy for him to 'have no urge' to view pornographic images?

994 It seems my self-control does not convince you This line suggests that Theseus must have made some dismissive gesture at this point.

Motives (995–1002)

Having pointed out that the burden of proof lies with Theseus (995), Hippolytus challenges three possible motives for assaulting Phaedra (just as Theseus had suggested three lines of defence, see 946–58).

- How tactful is Hippolytus in these lines and what impact might his arguments have on Theseus?

HIPPOLYTUS   Father, your anger and intensity of spirit are fearsome
But your case – though fine sounding – when unravelled,
Is anything but fine. I'm not smart at public speaking;
I'm more skilled in front of a few of my contemporaries.
This is only to be expected, since men who prove shallow   975
Among experts tend to be more inspiring in front of a mob.
Yet now this situation has arisen I feel compelled to speak out.
I will begin where you first tried to trap me,
Thinking you'd destroy me and I'd have no reply.
You see this sunlight and this earth.   980
In them there is no man of greater self-control,
Even if you should deny it, than me.
First, I know how to revere the gods, and to choose
Friends who are just in their dealings and would think it
Wrong to give wicked orders to their friends   985
Or treat them dishonourably. I am not one to mock
Those I consort with, father. I am constant to my friends,
Both present and absent. As for the one act you think
You've caught me doing, I am innocent:
To this moment of this day my body is untainted by sex.   990
I know nothing of it, save what I have heard
And seen in pictures; even these I have no urge
To look upon, because I keep my soul immaculate.
It seems my self-control does not convince you. So be it.
Yet it is for you to demonstrate how I was corrupted.   995
Did this woman's physical beauty surpass all others?
Or did I hope to possess your house by taking its heiress
As my wife? I would have been out of my mind –
In fact, completely stupid. Do you think
Royal power attracts men of sound sense?   1000
Hardly – those who delight in autocracy
Have already been ruined by it.

Hippolytus' pursuit of excellence (1003–7)

With the reference to 'best men' the Athenian audience would immediately recognise a statement of aristocratic ideals (see **'Hippolytus' plea of inexperience'**, page 84): aristocrats regularly trained and entered teams of horses at the 'Greek games', while the desire to 'take second place in the city' suggests a preference for influence behind the scenes rather than being champion of the mob (see 973–7, and compare Creon's defence in Sophocles' *Oedipus Tyrannus*).

- Do you think Hippolytus' approach to public life is related to his private quest for purity?

Hippolytus' oath (1013–20)

The power of an oath to sway a jury must not be underestimated: in Sophocles' *Oedipus* both Jocasta and the Chorus urge Oedipus to take Creon at his word primarily on the basis of 'the solemn oath he swears to heaven' (647, trans. Fagles). Hippolytus' oath is even more impressive as it includes a curse of self-destruction (*exōleia*).

- Why is it important for Hippolytus to insist he is innocent of not only the action but also the desire (1015–16)? What effect might this have on Theseus?

1020 If I am by nature wicked The absence of any witness and any further testimony from Phaedra (1009–12) compels Hippolytus to rest his defence on proving he is pure or chaste. The Greek words for 'wicked' and 'is by nature' or 'by birth' occur often in this scene (930, 933, 955, 1027, 1060, 1065 – see also 1169 and **'Hippolytus on trial'**, page 80).

1022 I may not speak further Though Hippolytus' oath to the Nurse (588–9) prevents him from disclosing the truth, there is nothing to stop him encouraging others to make further enquiries.

Sōphrosynē 4: good sense and self-control (1023–4)

Hippolytus uses the same verb (*sōphronein*) to mean both 'acted with good sense' and 'self-control'.

- What does Hippolytus mean by suggesting that the virtue of *sōphrosynē* can be practised by one who does not possess it (see especially **'*Sōphrosynē* 1'**, page 8, and 643n)?
- Compare Hippolytus' attitude to *sōphrosynē* here with his view of it at 73–5, 643 and 981–8: has his position changed? Has Phaedra succeeded in re-educating him (see **'*Sōphrosynē* 2'**, page 62)?

1028 smooth manner

- What might this phrase tell you about the way in which Hippolytus is perceived by others?

For my part I would choose to win and be first at
The Greek games, but to take second place in the city,
Always prospering with the best men as my friends.   1005
That way one has some power to take action, while
Absence of danger brings greater reward than sovereignty.
I have one thing more to say; the rest you have heard.
If I had a witness to my character
And were pleading my case with this woman still alive,   1010
Then, after a careful review of the facts,
You would see who the guilty are.
But now I swear to you, by Zeus, protector of oaths,
And by the solid earth beneath us,
I never touched your wife, nor ever wanted to,   1015
Nor ever entertained the idea.
May I perish without fame, my name forgotten,
[Without city or home, an exile left to wander the earth,]
May no sea, no land receive the flesh of my dead body,
If I am by nature wicked.   1020
What it was that she feared, that made her end her life,
I do not know. I may not speak further.
Though she lacked self-control, she acted with good sense;
I have self-control but did not use it well.
CHORUS   You have spoken well enough to overturn the charge,   1025
And by your oaths before the gods given a mighty pledge.
THESEUS   This fellow is a born spell-monger, a magician,
Convinced he'll win over my heart with his smooth manner,
After dishonouring the man who gave him life!
HIPPOLYTUS   I am equally amazed at you, father.   1030
If you were my son, and I your father, I would not have
Punished you with exile if you'd presumed to lay hands
Upon my wife – I would have killed you.

1038 A wandering exile on foreign soil Theseus repeats his words from 887. Exile to an ancient Greek was a fate worse than death since the sense of belonging to a city-state (*polis*) constituted a citizen's entire identity.

1044–5 the words of / The seers It was customary to consult seers (*manteis*) for an interpretation of any divine portents that might affect the outcome of a trial.

Three echoes

1. **1040 Time** This line tellingly echoes Phaedra's comment about Time always revealing the wicked (420–1).
2. **1042** At just the moment when Theseus is most instrumental in Aphrodite's plot, his words recall her proud boast of the extent of her power (3–4).
3. **1048** Much has been made of the differences between Theseus and Hippolytus, yet it is possible to detect deeper psychological similarities. Both reacted violently to shocking news, both wished that the world could be a simpler place (see **'Two voices'**, page 80) and both made spontaneous and irreversible judgements (see 878–87 and 621–6n). When Theseus stubbornly dismisses divination and omens with the phrase 'I bid them a very good day', he replicates Hippolytus' rejection of Aphrodite in the Prologue (110).

Hippolytus' resolve

Though aware that he will be destroyed by his oath of silence (1049–50), Hippolytus also reasons that it would be futile to break it (1051–2). This realisation signals the end of the *agōn*.

- Does Hippolytus' realisation make his resolve not to break his oath any less admirable?

1056 guest friend The rules of hospitality (*xenia*) were closely adhered to in ancient Greece. Under normal circumstances a traveller, as a kind of suppliant, could expect to be welcomed. Hippolytus fears that in exile he will be denied this refuge because of the charge against him.

Kakos (1060–7)

The Greek word for 'wicked' (*kakos* – see 12n) occurs three times in the space of eight lines (1060–7). For a young man who excluded the wicked from his 'untouched meadow' (75) the accusation is especially painful.

- Why might Hippolytus be more concerned by this accusation than the charge of rape?

THESEUS   How predictable your response!
Yet you will not die in the way you suggest –   1035
A swift death is too easy for a man in trouble. No,
You will drag out a life of pain, far from your native land,
A wandering exile on foreign soil.
[That is the price an impious man must pay.]
HIPPOLYTUS   Alas! What will you do? You won't let Time   1040
Speak on my behalf but drive me from the land?
THESEUS   Beyond the Pontic sea and the regions of Atlas
If I could; such is my loathing of you.
HIPPOLYTUS   Won't you test my oath, my pledge or the words of
The seers before banishing me from the land without trial?   1045
THESEUS   This tablet here needs no divination to convict you
Beyond any doubt. As for the birds that fly overhead,
I bid them a very good day.
HIPPOLYTUS   O you gods, why can't I loosen my tongue,
When those I worship are destroying me? No, I must not.   1050
I know of no way to convince those I must persuade
And I'd achieve nothing in breaking the oaths I swore.
THESEUS   Oh, your pious pride will be the death of me!
Leave the land of your fathers at once!
HIPPOLYTUS   Where shall I turn to in my misery? An exile   1055
On this charge, what guest friend can I visit now?
THESEUS   Go anywhere where men are welcome
Who rape women and make them partners in mischief.
HIPPOLYTUS   Ah! That strikes my heart. That brings me close to
Tears, if I seem so wicked and that's what you think of me.   1060
THESEUS   Back then was the time to show regret.
You should have considered the consequences
Before you dared abuse your father's wife.

Speech and silence 5 (1064–8)

The tension between speech and silence is acute at this point: the 'house', like Phaedra, the Chorus and Hippolytus himself, is silent.

- What does Theseus' response tell you about his attitude to the argument at this point?

1069–70 This curious sentiment is interpreted as self-love by Theseus.

- Are these lines evidence of self-love or self-pity? Why is Hippolytus unable to 'weep'?

My hateful birth! (1073–4)

Much as Phaedra knew that her status as a woman determined the way she was judged (399–400), Hippolytus interprets the references to being wicked as evidence of his father's prejudice against bastards (see **'Illegitimacy'**, page 78).

- This is the first line in the dialogue between father and son (1027–80) to which Theseus offers no response, and it prompts him to repeat his command to have Hippolytus removed. Why might Hippolytus' reference to his bastard status have angered Theseus?

1083 daughter of Leto Artemis (see 58). Hippolytus once again turns to the statue.

1086 Erechtheus See 146n.

Hippolytus' farewell (1081–92)

- 'I know the truth, but cannot make it known' (1082). Do you think Hippolytus believes there is a way of bringing the truth to light without breaking his oath?
- How might the actor playing Hippolytus present this speech? Would Hippolytus be vulnerable and distraught or defiant and proud?
- When does Theseus leave the stage? Would he stay to hear his son's farewell?

Review of Third Episode (747–1092)

The crucial decisions have been taken and Aphrodite's plan has nearly come to fruition in the course of a violent conflict between father and son conducted in the presence of Phaedra's corpse on the *ekkyklēma*.

- To what extent does Hippolytus' quest to avoid dying 'without fame' (*akleēs* – 1017) mirror Phaedra's attempt to avoid an act that is 'dishonourable' (*dusklea* – 399)?
- Has Hippolytus won back any sympathy from the audience after his earlier tirade?

HIPPOLYTUS O house, if only you could find a voice
To witness whether my nature is wicked. 1065
THESEUS How wise to seek refuge in a mute witness, but what
You did needs no words to proclaim your wickedness.
HIPPOLYTUS Alas.
If only I could stand back and see myself,
So I could weep at the injustice I am suffering. 1070
THESEUS It was always your way to worship yourself
Rather than be just and dutiful to your father.
HIPPOLYTUS O wretched mother! My hateful birth!
Let no friend of mine be born a bastard!
THESEUS Servants, drag him away. 1075
Didn't you hear me pronounce him banished?
HIPPOLYTUS Any one of them that touches me will regret it.
Force me from this land yourself if that is what you want.
THESEUS I will, if you won't obey my commands.
I feel no trace of pity at your banishment. 1080
HIPPOLYTUS My fate is fixed, it seems. How wretched I am:
I know the truth, but cannot make it known.
O daughter of Leto, most dear to me of all the gods,
Companion, fellow hunter – I am to be exiled from
Glorious Athens. Farewell to the city, 1085
To the land of Erechtheus. Farewell, plain of Trozen
– Such great happiness you offer to the young.
This is the last time I will look at or speak to you.
Come, my young companions from this land,
Talk to me as you send me on my way. 1090
You'll never see another man of greater self-control,
Even if my father doesn't think so.

THIRD *STASIMON* (1093–1132)

In light of the shock of Hippolytus' exile, the Chorus struggle to reconcile their belief in the benevolence of the gods (1093–4) with the injustice of his fate. Caution and adaptability seem vital (1102–6) if even a man of Hippolytus' virtue can suffer so (1107–11). Reflecting on the effects of his imminent departure (1112–24), the Chorus condemn the unfairness of the gods (1125–32).

Peripeteia

1099 Men's lives suffer change Plots in Greek tragedy are often framed by the idea of reversal of fortune (*peripeteia*). Heroic characters are laid low by a combination of their own mistakes (see 20n), the mistakes of others and the effect of changing 'circumstances' (1098). Perhaps the most striking example of *peripeteia* comes in Sophocles' *Ajax*, where the eponymous hero, renowned for valour on the battlefield, is outwitted by Odysseus and tricked by Athene into humiliating himself.

● How far is the *peripeteia* suffered by Phaedra and Hippolytus a result of circumstances beyond their control?

Pragmatism of the Chorus (1100–6)

These lines recall the philosophy of the Nurse (183–90).

● Do you think these strategies are effective ways of avoiding disaster?

1109–10 Greek Aphaea's / Brightest star Aphaea, a goddess worshipped on the nearby island of Aegina, was identified with Artemis. For the local goddess to be given such significance by being described as 'Greek' here elevates Hippolytus' stature as an ideal embodiment of Greek manhood and perhaps recalls his ambition to be 'first at / The Greek games' (1003–4).

1115 Dictynna The Chorus had used this alternative name for Artemis in the *parodos* (see 134–7n). The use of the name here is appropriate since it is linked to the Greek word for a hunting net (*diktyon*).

CHORUS   Whenever I think of the care the gods show us
A great weight of grief is lifted from me.
I cherish the hope of some understanding,   1095
Yet when I gaze on mortal deeds and fortunes
I am left wondering.
For circumstances turn, now this way, now that;
Men's lives suffer change, forever fluctuating.

If only destiny granted by the gods   1100
Could offer what I've prayed for:
Prosperity, good fortune and a heart untouched by pain!
May my thoughts be neither overstrict, nor falsely stamped.
May I share in tomorrow's good fortune
With an easy disposition,   1105
Always adapting to what the future brings.

For my mind is calm no longer when I gaze
On deeds that confound my hopes;
When we have seen Greek Aphaea's
Brightest star, have seen him hurled   1110
By his father's anger upon a foreign land.
O sands of the city's shore! Mountain grove,
Where with his swift-footed hounds
He used to hunt wild beasts
With holy Dictynna at his side!   1115

In praise of Hippolytus

After their appeal to the land where Hippolytus hunted (1112–15), the Chorus address him directly, lamenting his departure and the loss of his favourite activities: horse-racing (1116–18 – lines which echo Phaedra's fantasy at 221–4), playing the lyre (1119–20) and making offerings to Artemis ('Leto's daughter', 1121–2 – these lines poignantly recalling Hippolytus' offering of a garland to Artemis in the Prologue, 66–83).

1117–18 Venetia see 224n; **the Marsh** see 142n.

1119 Music from the lyre's frame The Greek for 'frame' (*antux*) is more commonly used of the handrail or rim (1209) on a chariot. Thus two activities dear to Hippolytus, linked by this word, become parallel elements in a harmonious lifestyle.

1126 Wretched mother Antiope/Hippolyta (see page v); in most versions of the myth she suffers a violent death soon after Hippolytus' birth.

The Graces (1129–32)

Commonly depicted as young girls with linked hands ('teamed together'), the Graces (*Charites*) were the patron goddesses of grace and beauty. They were also thought to encourage men and women into love and marriage.
- How do these lines and the mention of a 'bridal contest' (1123) offer a different perception of Hippolytus?

1131 Guilty of no madness Again the word *atē* is used (see 234n).
- Is this a fair assessment of Hippolytus?

Staging the third *stasimon*

Clues in the text suggest this *stasimon* was sung antiphonally by a Chorus of huntsmen (1093–9, 1107–15) and either the Chorus of women or a Chorus of younger girls (1100–6, 1116–32).
○ What would be the dramatic effect of this arrangement?

Review of the third *stasimon*

- How does this *stasimon* redirect the audience's sympathies after the tragedy of Phaedra earlier in the play?
- Do you think the Chorus idealise Hippolytus in this *stasimon*?

FOURTH EPISODE (1133–1242)

With attention focused on the implications of Hippolytus' exile, one of his attendants hurries to the palace to deliver news of a fresh disaster to Theseus.

No longer will you drive a team of colts from
Venetia, keeping the hooves of your trained
Horses tight to the race-track by the Marsh.
Music from the lyre's frame, never asleep
In your father's halls, will fill them no more   1120
And, deep in the forest, the haunts of Leto's daughter
          Will remain ungarlanded.
Your exile has robbed girls of the bridal contest
          For your bed.

In tears at your misfortune I will endure   1125
          A cursed fate. Wretched mother,
          Your child brought no joy.
          Ah, I rage at the gods! Alas, alas!
          Why did you Graces team together
               To send an unfortunate man,   1130
          Guilty of no madness, from this house,
               Away from his native land?

     Look! I see one of Hippolytus' attendants, heading
     With speed for the house, a grim look on his face.
MESSENGER   Where should I go, ladies,   1135
     To find Theseus, lord of this land? Tell me, if you know.
     Is he inside?
CHORUS   Here he is, coming out of the palace.
MESSENGER   Theseus, I bring news that will trouble you
     And your citizens, both those who dwell   1140
     In Athens and those in the land of Trozen.
THESEUS   What is it? Has some new misfortune
     Befallen these two neighbouring cities?

1144 Hippolytus is no more The dramatic impact of this news is intensified by an element of surprise: Poseidon's gift of three curses, the first of which Theseus used against his son soon after reading the tablet, has not been mentioned for more than 250 lines (see 878–80).

Theseus' initial reaction
Theseus seems sure the successful activation of the curse vindicates his judgement against Hippolytus. Yet his animated response also suggests a further underlying similarity to Hippolytus: the fact the curse *proves* Poseidon is Theseus' father may indicate prior uncertainty over who his real father was. Euripides cleverly exploits the variants of the Theseus myth (see page v) to add further psychological depth to the conflict between father and son.

Messenger speech
In most tragedies a messenger reports an important event which has happened away from the play's setting. His report is dramatised using vivid language, metaphor, simile and direct speech. This technique of storytelling, which draws on the oral epic tradition that inspired the *Iliad* and *Odyssey*, offers considerable opportunities to the actor.

Hippolytus' popularity
Prior to this speech there has been very little evidence to suggest Hippolytus is popular outside his circle of friends. He is aloof (see 90n and **'Hippolytus' plea of inexperience'**, page 84) and his lack of ambition (1003–7) does not require him to court popularity.
● Is Euripides' characterisation of Hippolytus consistent?
● Consider Hippolytus' actions as described in lines 1158–72: how might they inspire admiration?

1167 Chariot rail The double meaning of *antux* (see 1119n) helps reinforce Hippolytus' artistry as a horseman since his taking up of the reins echoes the plucking of the lyre-strings. His confident handling of the four-horse team is further emphasised at 1171–2.

1169 if my nature is wicked This phrase recalls the central accusation in the *agōn* between Theseus and Hippolytus (see 1020n, 1065 and **'Kakos'**, page 88). The prayer to Zeus as protector of oaths (see 1013) is Hippolytus' last act before beginning his fateful journey.
● How fitting do you find Hippolytus' valedictory words? What do they reveal about his character?

1175 Argos and Epidaurus The two major towns to the north-west of Trozen.

MESSENGER   Hippolytus is no more, near to death; he still looks
   On the light, but his life hangs on a small tilt of the scales.   1145
THESEUS   Who did this? Did he provoke someone's hostility
   By violating his wife, as he did his father's?
MESSENGER   His own chariot destroyed him, and the curse
   Which with your lips you laid upon your son
   When you prayed to your father, lord of the sea.   1150
THESEUS   Gods! Poseidon! By answering my prayers you have
   Proved yourself my father! So how did he die? Tell me.
   How did the trap of Justice close on him for his offence to me?
MESSENGER   We were by the wave-beaten shore, grooming the
   Horses' manes with combs, in tears. Someone came   1155
   To tell us you'd condemned Hippolytus to pitiful exile,
   That he would never again set foot in this land.
   Then *he* joined us on the shore – on foot behind him a
   Vast crowd of friends and men of similar age to him –
   And shared the same tale of tears. At some point   1160
   He stopped his lamentations and said: 'Why be foolish?
   I must obey my father. Get my horses ready, boys,
   Fasten them to the chariot. This city is no longer mine.'
   Then everyone set to work, and quicker than a man could
   Speak we had prepared the horses and brought them to   1165
   Stand close by their master. He took up the reins from the
   Chariot rail and mounted, his feet slipping into the foot-rests.
   First, he addressed the gods with hands spread wide:
   'Zeus, may I die if my nature is wicked!
   Let my father come to realise that he dishonours me,   1170
   Whether dead or still alive.' Saying this he took the
   Whip and in one movement flicked it over the horses.
   We attendants followed our master beside the chariot,
   Keeping close by the bridles, along the road
   That leads straight to Argos and Epidaurus.   1175

1176 A promontory North-west of Trozen is a rugged promontory (now called Cape Nísiza) where the sea opens out into the Saronic Gulf, affording views north to 'Sciron's coast' – the cliffs west of Megara, named after the villain killed by Theseus (see 967), which extend as far as the Isthmus of Corinth, and west to 'Asclepius' rock'. The exact location of the rock is unknown but likely to be Epidaurus, a cult centre of Asclepius, a god of healing with whom Hippolytus was later associated.

Hippolytus drives his chariot; Poseidon's bull is just visible beneath the horses. Red-figure volute-krater (detail), attributed to the Darius painter, c. 350–325 BC.

Poseidon's bull

As a symbol of masculinity and sexual aggression, the bull seems an appropriate instrument of Hippolytus' demise. Interwoven with this symbolism are echoes of Phaedra (the association of the bull with Poseidon is evident from the story of her parents, Minos and Pasiphaë, see 332n and page v) and Aphrodite (the 'foam' – *aphros* – from which the bull emerges recalls the myth of her birth from the sea, see 408n).

Sea imagery 2

Pursued by the bull, Hippolytus is described as the helmsman of a ship ('captain', 1201; 'helm', 1202) as he attempts to guide his horses to safety ('as a sailor pulls his oar', 1197).

● How might Hippolytus' struggle to direct his team in the face of an altogether more powerful force be an appropriate metaphor for his life?

Then we headed into deserted country. A promontory lies
Beyond our borders, facing what becomes the Saronic Gulf.
It was here an echoing shudder of the earth, like
Zeus' thunder, rose to a deep roar, terrifying to hear.
The horses raised their heads to the heavens,   1180
Pricked up their ears; violent fear gripped us.
We wondered where the sound was coming from.
Then as we cast our eyes over the sea-lashed shore we
Saw an unearthly sight: a vast wave stood fixed in the sky,
Blocking my view of Sciron's coast, hiding too the isthmus   1185
And Asclepius' rock. Then, swelling up, spitting
Thick foam all around as the sea was blasted upwards,
It made for the shore, to where the four-horse chariot stood.
As this wave, a mountainous wall of water, broke,
It revealed a bull, a savage monster.   1190
The whole earth was filled with its bellowing;
The echo that resounded made us tremble and,
As we looked, the spectacle seemed more than
Our eyes could bear. At once the horses were seized
By terrible panic and my master, well accustomed   1195
To their ways, held the reins tight in both hands
And pulled them, as a sailor pulls his oar, letting
The reins take the weight of his body. Yet the horses
Champed the fire-forged bits in their jaws,
Bearing him onwards by sheer force,   1200
Paying no heed to their captain's hand, their harness
Or the well-built chariot. Whenever he steadied the helm,
Guiding his course to softer ground,
The bull would rear in front of him,
Forcing him to turn back,   1205
Driving the four-horse team into a frenzy of fear.

1208 in silence A sinister detail. After the earlier 'bellowing' (1191) the stealth of the bull is eerie and supernatural.

1214 caught by a knot tied fast Like the wrestling metaphor (see 6n, 176n, 647n), the image of the 'knot' helps to illustrate a central theme in the play, that mankind's ambitions are frequently thwarted by uncontrollable forces. Phaedra's metaphorical 'knot / These words have tied' (see 648–9 and **'Speech and silence 2'**, page 58) is here surpassed by the literal knot that destroys Hippolytus.

Tragic irony (1216–18)
The literal meaning of Hippolytus' name is 'releaser of horses'. Ironically his beloved team of horses drag him over the rocks before he can release them. The dramatic re-enactment of the actual words of the tragic hero was a common feature in messenger speeches (see the dying words of Pentheus as reported by the Messenger in Euripides' *Bacchae*).

1225–9 Throughout his speech the Messenger's perspective has been clear, if understated: Hippolytus is not 'wicked' (*kakos*, see 12n and page 88) but 'honourable' (the Greek word *esthlos* is the direct opposite of *kakos*). His demise is Theseus' doing, not a consequence of his own actions (see 1148–50, 1156–7).

1227 Even if every woman in the world hanged herself This heartfelt sentiment may also be intended as a veiled criticism of Theseus' rashness.

1228 Ida The Messenger probably has in mind the famous Mount Ida just outside Troy. However, there was a mountain of the same name in Crete.

Review of the Messenger speech
- How does Euripides convey the impression of an eye-witness account?
- Does the Messenger's earlier mention of what has happened to Hippolytus (1144–5) heighten or lessen the dramatic impact of the speech?
○ Consider ways of staging the speech. Would the actor face the audience or speak directly to Theseus? How might he use gestures to illustrate his story? How might his emotions affect his report?

Theseus' ambivalence (1232–5)
A sense of 'respect for the gods' who protect family ties prevents Theseus from expressing emotion.

When they careered towards the rocks, driven out
Of their wits, the bull would draw near in silence,
Gaining on the chariot until, finally, he touched the rail,
Overturned it and dashed the wheel rims on a rock.   1210
Then everything was confusion. The spokes split
From the wheels, the linchpins sprang from the axles;
The master himself was tangled in the reins and dragged,
Still caught by a knot tied fast, his head battered
On the rocks, his body shattered. He cried out in words   1215
That were awful to hear: 'Hold fast, my horses,
Reared in my stables, don't destroy me! O, how bitter
My father's curse! Who will rescue a noble man?'
Many would have helped, but we'd been outpaced
And left behind. Then he was freed from the reins   1220
That bound him – I don't know how – and fell,
Still breathing for the short time left to him. The horses
Vanished, with the gruesome apparition of the bull,
Into the rocky earth – I don't know where.
My lord, I'm only a slave in your house,   1225
But I'd never believe your son is wicked,
Even if every woman in the world hanged herself
And covered the pines on Ida with writing;
I know he is an honourable man.

CHORUS   Alas! New disasters mingle with old.   1230
There is no release from destiny, from what must be.

THESEUS   Out of hate for the man who has suffered this
I took pleasure at these words, but out of respect for the gods,
And for him, since he is my blood, I now feel
Neither pleasure nor pain at this catastrophe.   1235

MESSENGER   What, then? Should we bring the poor man here?
Or how else can we help you?

Review of the Fourth Episode (1133–1242)

In this episode Theseus is utterly dispassionate about Hippolytus, never once calling him 'son'. His anger was understandable in the previous episode, but the Messenger speech has had the effect of drawing sympathy away from him, isolating him in his contempt for Hippolytus.

● What impression do you get of the character of the Messenger?
● What does Theseus' response to the Messenger speech (1232–5, 1240–2) suggest about his character?
● How has this episode built on the positive impression given of Hippolytus in the third *stasimon*?

FOURTH *STASIMON* (1243–58)

As the Messenger leaves the stage to bring the fatally wounded Hippolytus in, the Chorus sing a short ode to Aphrodite and Eros ('the bright-feathered one'). The placement of this ode to Aphrodite just before the appearance of Artemis mirrors the Prologue, where the ode to Artemis follows the appearance of Aphrodite.

● How does the depiction of Aphrodite and Eros here compare with their earlier portrayal in the first *stasimon* (516–45)?
● Why do the Chorus pay their respects to Aphrodite's power so soon after praising her victim and raging against the gods (1128)?

Think about it; if you take my advice you won't
Be brutal towards your son in his misfortune.

THESEUS Bring him here. He denies he violated my bed,   1240
But once I have him here before me I will prove his guilt,
Weighing his words and this misfortune sent by the gods.

CHORUS   Cypris, you command the unyielding hearts
                         Of gods and mortals,
                     You and the bright-feathered one,   1245
                 Swift of wing, who encircles them,
                     Attacks them from all sides.
                     Hovering over the land,
                     Over the roaring salt sea,
             Eros maddens and beguiles his victims,   1250
             Attacks them on radiant gold wings:
         Young beasts of the mountains and the seas,
                 All the earth nourishes
             And the burning sun beholds,
                     And men;   1255
             With the honour due to a queen,
                 You alone hold sway
             Over all of these, Cypris.

EXODOS (1259–1452)
Exodos is the term for both the exit of the Chorus and the final Episode.

Deus ex machina
Often in Euripides a deity is brought on near the end to resolve the action and to impart information that cannot be known by human characters. The ancient Greek theatre used a crane called the *mēkhanē* to swing immortals high into view, probably onto the roof of the *skēnē* (see page 123).

○ Consider ways of staging the sudden appearance of the goddess in a modern production.

The presence of Artemis
Artemis (see page 4) appears on the *mēkhanē*, carrying the bow and arrows (see 1404, and image, page 106) that make her instantly recognisable. Her presence here mirrors that of Aphrodite in the Prologue.

● What issues do you expect Artemis to deal with here?

1259 Aegeus See page v. Despite the evidence of the curse, Theseus is still known as his son (see notes on Theseus, pages 4 and 96).

Nobility 1
The range of Greek words for 'noble' and 'nobility' generates ambiguity. When Theseus is described as a 'noble son' (1259) the word is *eupatridēn*, which means nothing more than noble lineage (the Chorus used the same word for Theseus in the *parodos*, 145), and Artemis makes it clear (1272) that he can no longer be counted 'among good men' (*agathoi* – a word with both aristocratic and moral connotations). Hippolytus earlier used a form of *agathos* to describe himself as 'noble' (1218), and similarly the word *gennaios* (see **'Nobility 2'**, page 116), used for Phaedra's 'nobility' (1277), suggests dignified conduct in keeping with her station (contrast the 'nobility' of the first adulteress, 401–5n).

1267 ruin The Greek word *atē* denotes not only a delusion but also the ruin that follows it (see 234n, 1131n).

1270–1 lifting yourself / Out of this suffering Artemis' suggestion picks up the Chorus's longing for escape in the second *stasimon* (see 709–18).

1277–82 After Phaedra's own doubts about her character and Hippolytus' condemnation of her (593–644), this is the first time her moral struggle is officially acknowledged and praised.

1281 She did not consent
● Re-read lines 507–11. How do Artemis' words influence your interpretation of Phaedra in those lines?

ARTEMIS	I command you, noble son of Aegeus,	
	To listen: it is I, Artemis,	1260
	Daughter of Leto, who address you.	
	Theseus, wretched man, why do you	
	Take pleasure in this,	
	When you have sinfully killed your son,	
	When your wife's lying words	1265
	Have convinced you of what was not proved?	
	What is clear is the ruin you have caused.	
	Sink your body in the depths	
	Of the earth for shame,	
	Or rise in flight, lifting yourself	1270
	Out of this suffering.	
	You have no share in life among good men.	

Listen, Theseus, to the catalogue of your troubles.
It will do no good, and it will cause you pain.
I have come to reveal the purity of your son's mind,   1275
So he may die with a good name, and to explain your wife's
Passion – or, in a way, her nobility. For she was stricken
With pangs from the goddess whom we, who delight in
Virginity, most hate, and she fell in love with your son.
She tried to overcome Cypris by strength of will;   1280
She did not consent to her Nurse's schemes,
Yet they destroyed her. It was the Nurse who forced
An oath from your son and then revealed her mistress' sickness.
He, quite rightly, chose not to do as she asked,
And, even when abused by you, being honourable,   1285
He did not betray the oath that bound him.
Phaedra, fearing she might be exposed,
Wrote a deceiving letter and with her lies destroyed
Your son. But you believed her.

Theseus' guilt

Artemis condemns Theseus' failure to deal justly with the charge against Hippolytus (see 1035–48). Lines 1299–1301 deliberately recall Hippolytus' similar complaint (1044–5). Yet the principal charge against Theseus concerns his impulsive use of the curse. Poseidon is forced to carry out his promise, becoming an accomplice to a murder that brings pollution (as Theseus later admits, see 1430–3). With the realisation of his guilt, Theseus' *peripeteia* (see page 92) is complete.

Artemis fires her bow. Attic red-figure bell-krater (detail), c. 470 BC.

1295 You wicked man The Greek copies the very words used by Theseus to describe Hippolytus (947).

1307 There is a law among the gods In *Iliad* xxii Zeus considers saving Hector in his duel with Achilleus, and is prevented from doing so by the anger of Athene and respect for the inevitability of predetermined *moira* (destiny, lot or portion of life). The Chorus have shown respect for this inevitability (1231), but the 'law' of non-interference whereby gods take turns to exert their will on mortals here seems to have replaced the traditional concept of destiny.

● What impression do you get of the relationship between gods and mortals in the play?

Theseus forgiven – dual causality

Theseus is indisputably at fault for Hippolytus' downfall, but Artemis also excuses him as he had no choice but to act out Aphrodite's will. For each key event in the play two explanations can be offered: the enactment of divine will and the result of human failings. This dual causality is apparent throughout and is the source of much of its ambiguity and subtlety.

● How comforting do you think Theseus would find Artemis' absolution?
● 'No human character in the play is wholly innocent or wholly guilty.' How true is this statement of Phaedra, the Nurse, Hippolytus and Theseus?

1317 I too suffer pain

● What signs of grief has Artemis given in her speech so far?

THESEUS Alas. 1290

ARTEMIS Does this account wound you, Theseus? Be quiet.
You will be sorrier when you hear what follows.
You know the three curses you had, promised you
By your father? One of these you used against your son,
You wicked man; you should have kept it for an enemy. 1295
Your father, the sea-lord, meaning well,
Gave what he had promised, as he was obliged to.
It is you who have plainly done wrong – to him and to me:
You did not stop to consider your son's oath,
Or consult the seers' words; you did not 1300
Test his case or allow time for investigation.
Instead, more quickly than you should have,
You let fly curses at your son and caused his death.

THESEUS Mistress, I want to die.

ARTEMIS What you did was terrible, yet you can still 1305
Find forgiveness. For Cypris willed this to happen,
To satisfy her anger. There is a law among the gods:
No god will block another's will.
Instead, we always stand aside. Know this well:
Had I not feared Zeus I never would have incurred 1310
The shame of allowing the mortal I loved most
To die. But – firstly – ignorance of your mistake
Acquits you of doing wrong.
Then, your wife's death destroyed the chance of
Questioning her and so you were convinced. 1315
This misfortune has shattered you more than any,
But I too suffer pain. The gods do not rejoice when
Good men die, though we do destroy the wicked –
Themselves, their children and their homes.

Hippolytus' entrance

The Greek verb in 1320 suggests that Hippolytus is able to walk, but it is clear from the text (1332, 1337–41) that he requires attendants to support him on either side.

Hippolytus' lament (1325–67)

Despite the *peripeteia* (see page 92) he has suffered, Hippolytus remains defiant, referring to Theseus' actions as 'unjust' (1327) and calling the gods to witness his unfair treatment. He also expresses bitterness towards his own horses. The metre of the lament is deliberately erratic to emphasise Hippolytus' pain.

Olōla (1329)

The Greek word translated here as 'I am finished' literally means 'I have been destroyed'. It is spoken four times in the *exodos*, three times by Hippolytus (1329, 1429, 1443) and once by Theseus (1389).

1340 Lift me with care The Greek recalls Phaedra's request to be lifted up on her sick-bed (191). The power exerted over both characters by Aphrodite is thus emphasised.

o If you were directing the play, how might you help the audience to notice this parallel?

Zeus

Unlike Aphrodite, Artemis and Poseidon, Zeus plays no direct part in the drama. Yet it is to Zeus that the human characters make their most significant appeals (593, 660–1, 877, 1343) and even the gods fear him (1310). Although Zeus is the ultimate moral arbiter, Hippolytus sees his failure to intervene to confirm his goodness as negligence, especially after his impressive oaths (see 1013, 1169).

1344 the devout one Hippolytus uses the ambiguous *semnos*, a word the Servant had used to describe a 'proud' goddess (see 90n).

Sōphrosynē 5 (1345)

A further, literal meaning of *sōphrosynē* is 'safe thinking'. Even at the moment when it is most obvious that his virtue hasn't saved him, Hippolytus' continued belief in his own, perhaps peculiar, sense of the word is impressive (see '*Sōphrosynē* 1' and 'Self-control', both page 8).

CHORUS	Here he comes, poor man,	1320
	His young flesh, his fair hair disfigured.	
	O the agonies of this house!	
	A double blow has been dealt,	
	Grief from the gods now grips this house.	

HIPPOLYTUS	Ah! Ah!	1325
	I am wretched, disfigured	
	By the unjust curses	
	Of an unjust father.	
	I am finished, already dead!	
	Pain courses through my head,	1330
	A spasm shoots through my brain.	
	Stop! I must rest my failing body.	
	Ah!	
	My team, hateful to me now,	
	Reared by my own hand,	1335
	You destroyed me, you killed me.	
	Ah! In heaven's name, be gentle, servants,	
	When you touch my injured body.	
	Who stands by my right side?	
	Lift me with care, be gentle	1340
	When you carry my body, ill-fated,	
	Cursed by my father's fault!	
	Zeus, Zeus, do you see this?	
	I, the devout one, the god-fearer,	
	The one who surpassed all others in self-control,	1345
	In full awareness I go to Hades,	
	My life utterly destroyed.	

1348 my reverence towards men Reverence (*eusebeia*) is usually directed towards gods, but Hippolytus uses it to describe his transactions with 'men' – a subtle hint at the error in his conduct.

1348 in vain This phrase reinforces the idea, prevalent in the play, that divine power renders human actions futile (the same Greek word, *allōs*, is used earlier by the Chorus, see **'A cautionary note'**, page 46).

1352 Death the Healer The idea of death as a remedy for suffering was beginning to take root in Greek thought, particularly in the Eleusinian Mysteries (see 25n). In Plato's *Phaedo*, Socrates, just before death, claims to owe the sacrifice of a cockerel to the healing god Asclepius, with whom Hippolytus was later associated (see 1176n).

1357 stain of some evil For the third time in the play (see 331–6, 807–10) the idea of an inherited curse is employed to explain misfortune. Whereas Phaedra has specific grounds for considering her family cursed, Theseus and Hippolytus, blind to the errors of their ways, are merely guessing.

Review of Hippolytus' lament (1325–67)
Much of the drama in the lament stems from Hippolytus' agony. His longing for death is, however, driven as much by disillusionment as by physical pain. Unaware of the true cause of his demise, he blames his father (1327–8, 1356) and appeals to Zeus (1343) in disbelief that his virtue (not to mention his oaths, see page 86) could be overlooked. Yet despite his claim to be 'the god-fearer' (1344) there are hints in his lament (1344n, 1348n) of what has caused his downfall.

● Which of the following words best describes the tone of Hippolytus' lament: *naive, defiant, idealistic, angry, bewildered*?
Theseus remains on stage throughout the lament and does not address his son until 1389.
● What might this suggest about Theseus' emotional state?
○ How might the actor playing Theseus respond physically during the lament?

Hippolytus and Artemis (1368–87)
Hippolytus' special relationship with Artemis has been remarked upon by Aphrodite (14–18) and, obliquely, by Theseus (936–7), and Hippolytus is temporarily revived (1370–2) by her presence. Her position on the *mēkhanē* (see **'Deus ex machina'**, page 104) means she remains invisible to him throughout the scene (see 81).

1368 harnessed The metaphor is appropriate: not only was Hippolytus physically harnessed to his horses, but Iole was 'Yoked' (the Greek word is the same) to Heracles in servitude to Aphrodite (see 535n).

In my reverence towards men I laboured in vain.
Ah! Ah!
Pain upon pain comes over me – 1350
Release me, poor wretch –
Let Death the Healer come to me.
Finish me off, finish me, in my misery.
I long for a double-edged blade
To cut through and lay my life to rest. 1355
O my father's wretched curse!
The stain of some evil,
Inherited from ancestors of old,
Has burst its bounds;
Unrelenting it makes for me – 1360
Why me?
I am guilty of no wrongdoing.
Oh! What shall I say?
How can I rid my life of this suffering
So it no longer causes pain? 1365
If only the black night, the force of Hades,
Could lay me to rest, in my misery!

ARTEMIS   Unhappy boy, harnessed to such a misfortune!
The nobility of your mind has destroyed you.
HIPPOLYTUS   Breath of fragrance divine! Even in my suffering 1370
I sense your presence and the pain in my body is
Lightened. The goddess Artemis is here, in this place.

1373–99 This passage of *stichomythia* (see also 86–104, 303–49, 579–92, 1428–42) is the only one to involve three characters rather than two.

1373–80 In language that recalls his prayer to Artemis (66–83) Hippolytus reminds the goddess of his devotion (1376, 1378–9) as he looks for sympathy (1374).

● How sympathetic do you find Artemis' responses in these lines?

Anagnōrisis (1381)

In *The Art of Poetry*, Aristotle analyses *anagnōrisis* ('discovery', 'realisation') as an essential component of any drama. It is further defined as 'a change from ignorance to knowledge'. Hippolytus' realisation of who is really responsible for his death brings the drama to its close.

Sōphrosynē 6 (1383)

In the Prologue Aphrodite criticised Hippolytus for keeping company that was 'more than mortal' (18). Artemis explains that it is his 'self-control' that 'angered' Aphrodite. As a final comment on this complex word, it is worth considering that Hippolytus seemingly aspires to emulate a divine virtue – the kind of austerity and purity exhibited by Artemis in this scene (see especially 1375, 1419–21) – and that this endeavour to be 'more than mortal' is the grounds of the charge of *hybris* (see page 40).

● Review all the notes on *sōphrosynē* (pages 8, 62, 84, 86, 108); has your opinion of the best translations of the word changed (see page 62 for the list of possible translations)?

1384 the three of us Hippolytus may be referring to himself, Theseus and Artemis, in which case Artemis' reply (1385) corrects the mistake.

1388 I pity you This could be seen as a climactic moment in the play: Hippolytus, often accused of being cold or aloof, displays genuine emotion (see also 1386) towards his father.

1397 You would have killed me Hippolytus appears to understand the inevitability of Theseus' anger, and with it the illusory nature of free will (see **'Theseus forgiven'**, page 106).

1398 tripped me The final instance of the verb *sphallō* (see also 6, 97, 176, 253, 647 and notes). As on its first occurrence, the wrestling metaphor is used to illustrate the effect of divine intervention on human actions.

1399 curse the gods For the first time in the play Hippolytus shows an inclination to criticise the divine order as a whole, though he does not go so far as to deliver the curse.

● Has Hippolytus' *anagnōrisis* (see above) significantly affected his attitude to Theseus, to the gods and to his own pursuit of virtue?

● Does Hippolytus show any repentance for his denial of Aphrodite's power?

ARTEMIS Unhappy boy, she is – the goddess dearest to you.

HIPPOLYTUS Do you see me, mistress – the pitiful state I am in?

ARTEMIS I do. Yet I may not shed tears. 1375

HIPPOLYTUS Your huntsman, your attendant, is no more.

ARTEMIS No, but even in death you remain dear to me.

HIPPOLYTUS The steward of your horses, guardian of your
Image, is no more.

ARTEMIS Cypris devised it so, the mischief-maker. 1380

HIPPOLYTUS Ah! Now I know which goddess has destroyed me.

ARTEMIS She found fault in your failure to pay her honour,
And your self-control angered her.

HIPPOLYTUS Cypris, I realise now, has destroyed the three of us.

ARTEMIS Your father, you, and – thirdly – his wife. 1385

HIPPOLYTUS I begin to grieve for my father's misfortune.

ARTEMIS He was deceived by the scheming of a god.

HIPPOLYTUS My poor father, I pity you for these misfortunes.

THESEUS I am finished, my son. Life holds
No pleasure for me now. 1390

HIPPOLYTUS Despite your fault I suffer more
For you than for myself.

THESEUS If only I could die instead of you, my son.

HIPPOLYTUS Those gifts of your father Poseidon brought no joy!

THESEUS How I wish that curse had never crossed my lips! 1395

HIPPOLYTUS Why? You were so angry then
You would have killed me anyway.

THESEUS The gods tripped me. My judgement was deluded.

HIPPOLYTUS If only men could curse the gods!

Artemis' final speech (1400–21)

Whatever sympathy she feels for her protégé, Artemis will not allow blasphemy in her presence. Before departing she makes predictions concerning the destinies of the principal characters.

Adonis (1404–5)

Although not named, the 'mortal man' Aphrodite 'holds most dear' is most likely Adonis, a youth of exceptional beauty, loved by Persephone, the queen of the underworld, and Aphrodite. In most versions of the tale he was killed not by 'arrows' but by a boar. In later writers Artemis is held responsible for his death.

The cult of Hippolytus (1406–10)

Euripides often links his version of a story to a local festival or cult, providing the original audience with a sense of continuity between the legendary past and the present. In addition to gods, the ancient Greeks worshipped heroes, often dedicating sacred ground to them within their sanctuaries. The cult of Hippolytus originated in Trozen, but spread to Athens; inscriptional evidence suggests there was a precinct to Hippolytus within the temple of Cypris (see 28–31n).

- Artemis assures Hippolytus, a symbol of chastity, undying fame. His worship will mark a rite of passage for women 'before their wedding day'. Do you consider this an appropriate accolade?

Speech and silence 6 (1412–13)

Phaedra's dilemma (see **'Reputation'**, page 34) centred on her need to justify her actions yet keep them concealed. Ironically, it is 'Phaedra's love', not her 'noble acts' (397) that will 'not fall forgotten into silence'.

The distance between gods and men

Commenting on this scene, the scholar W.S. Barrett concludes: 'The human conflict is resolved by death; the Olympian conflict continues, irresoluble.' Artemis began by focusing on her arch-rival Aphrodite before proceeding to resolve the human situation. She shows some sympathy for Hippolytus (1368, 1373, 1407) but ignores his allusions to their special companionship (1376–80) and is eager to leave when her favourite mortal is about to die (1419–21). Hippolytus, though faithful to the last, remarks on the 'ease' (1423) with which she leaves him. As with the forgiveness of Theseus (see page 106), it is cold comfort to learn that 'It is natural for men to fall into error when gods will it' (1416).

- How does this scene (1368–1425) emphasise the gulf between gods and men?

1429 the gates of the underworld See 53–4.

ARTEMIS Enough! Not even in the gloom below the earth   1400
   Shall the angry cruelty of the goddess Cypris,
   Which she willed on you, go unavenged, thanks to
   Your piety and the goodness of your mind.
   For with these unerring arrows I myself will
   Take vengeance on the mortal man she holds most dear.   1405
   To atone for these sufferings I will grant you,
   Unfortunate youth, the highest honours in the city
   Of Trozen: before their wedding day unmarried girls
   Will cut a lock of hair for you, and you forevermore
   Will win from them a bounty of sad tears.   1410
   When maidens compose songs
   They will think always of you, and Phaedra's love
   Will not fall forgotten into silence.
   Son of old Aegeus, take your son in your arms,
   Hold him close. For, though unwittingly, you killed him.   1415
   It is natural for men to fall into error when gods will it.
   My advice to you, Hippolytus: do not hate your father.
   This is your destiny, to die like this.
   Farewell. I may not look upon the dead;
   The last breath of the dying must not taint my sight.   1420
   I see you are already close to that sad end.
HIPPOLYTUS Farewell as you depart, blessed maid.
   With ease you leave our long companionship.
   At your request I end my quarrel with my father,
   Obedient to your commands as always.   1425
   Ah! Darkness begins to steal over my eyes.
   Hold me, father, lay my body straight.
THESEUS Oh, my son, what are you doing to me? Oh misfortune!
HIPPOLYTUS I am finished. I see the gates of the underworld.
THESEUS Are you leaving me with hands defiled?   1430
HIPPOLYTUS No. I acquit you of this murder.

Hippolytus' forgiveness

Although freed of moral responsibility as a 'pawn' of the gods, Theseus is still defiled by 'blood-guilt' (see 306n) since he invoked the curse against his son. In Athenian law the victim before death could free his killer from the consequences of murder.

Nobility 2 (1436)

Artemis spoke of the 'nobility' of Hippolytus' mind (1369) and Theseus goes further in calling him 'noble' (*gennaios*). In both cases the Greek words suggest nobility by birth (see **'Nobility 1'**, page 104), which suggests Hippolytus has at last rid himself of the slur of illegitimacy (see pages 78 and 90). This line also suggests that Hippolytus has finally found how to manifest his virtue in a way that others can understand.

1440–1 as fortunate as this / With your true-born sons
● Do you think there is a note of bitterness in these lines?

Stichomythia (1428–42)

● Compare this passage of *stichomythia* with those earlier in the play (86–104, 303–49, 579–92, 1373–99): how is each of the scenes made more dramatic by single-line dialogue and what light is shed on the conflicts and emotions of the characters?

1444 cover my face As he dies, Hippolytus' final request serves as a reminder of his modesty (see also 935n).

1445 Pallas A title of Athene, patron goddess of Athens.

1447–8 The play ends as it began – with a tribute to Aphrodite's power.

Review of the *exodos*

● Artemis appears on the *mēkhanē*, whereas Aphrodite appeared on stage. How might this reflect the difference between the two goddesses and the way they affect human beings?
● How have your perceptions of Hippolytus and Theseus been altered in this scene?
● Which character deserves to be considered as the central tragic character in the play: Phaedra, Hippolytus or Theseus?
● In *The Art of Poetry* Aristotle suggests that Greek tragic plays were designed to generate emotions of pity and fear in the audience; how might these emotions be generated by this play?

Epilogue (1449–52)

● Some scholars think these lines were added by actors and contribute little to the play. Do you think they add anything to the drama that has unfolded on stage?

THESEUS What are you saying? You release me
From this blood-guilt?

HIPPOLYTUS Yes. I call Artemis, whose bow
Brings death, as witness.   1435

THESEUS Dear son, how noble you have shown
Yourself to your father!

HIPPOLYTUS Farewell, father – my long farewell to you!

THESEUS I weep for the piety, the goodness of your mind.

HIPPOLYTUS Pray that you may be as fortunate as this   1440
With your true-born sons!

THESEUS Don't leave me now, my son. Endure.

HIPPOLYTUS My endurance is ended. I am finished, father.
Quickly, cover my face with your robe.

THESEUS O famous boundaries of Athens and Pallas,   1445
What a man is stolen from you!
How wretched I am. Cypris, how well I will remember
Your cruel acts.

CHORUS   This shared grief has come
Upon all citizens without warning.   1450
Often will tears be shed in abundance.
Tales of great men deserve greater sorrow.

Theseus and Hippolytus. University of Utah production, 1997.

Synopsis of the play

PROLOGUE (1–117)

The goddess Aphrodite states her intention to punish Hippolytus for failing to honour her. She is angered by his exclusive devotion to Artemis. Her plan against Hippolytus was previously set in motion when he left Trozen to visit Athens, where his stepmother Phaedra was made to fall in love with him. Theseus, forced to absent himself from Athens for one year after the murder of his cousins, the Pallantides, is now living in Trozen but is away consulting an oracle and Aphrodite intends to bring her plan to fruition when he returns.

Hippolytus enters with his huntsmen. After a devout prayer to Artemis, he is advised by a Servant to pay greater respect to Aphrodite. Hippolytus dismisses the advice, whereupon the Servant prays to Aphrodite on his behalf.

PARADOS (118–69)

The Chorus of Trozenian women report the news they have heard about Phaedra's sickness. They speculate as to what has caused it. As the ode ends they catch sight of Phaedra and her Nurse appearing outdoors.

FIRST EPISODE (170–515)

Phaedra's Nurse complains bitterly about the tiresome task of looking after an invalid who shows no sign of convalescing. After assuring the Chorus of her ignorance, the Nurse begins to interrogate Phaedra, determined to find the cause of her sickness. After the mention of Hippolytus' name draws an involuntary reaction from Phaedra, the Nurse supplicates her mistress and forces the truth from her. She is horrified by what she hears.

Phaedra proceeds to justify her conduct, explaining how she attempted to resist her feelings for her stepson and condemning the first adulteress and the trouble she has brought on all womankind. The Nurse, alarmed by her mistress's resolve to die, now argues that Phaedra should give in to her passion. Phaedra rejects this advice but an argument ensues and in her weakened state she cannot prevent the Nurse's attempts to find a cure.

FIRST *STASIMON* (516–45)

The Chorus sing an ode honouring Eros and Aphrodite, citing Iole and Semele as examples of mortals who have been destroyed by their power.

SECOND EPISODE (546–708)

A commotion is heard within the palace and Phaedra realises that the Nurse has divulged her secret to Hippolytus. The Nurse has forced Hippolytus to swear an oath of secrecy. Hippolytus enters in a rage. He condemns womankind and threatens to return upon the arrival of Theseus to observe the behaviour of Phaedra and the Nurse. After a brief lament, Phaedra turns on the Nurse, blaming her for the perilous situation she now finds herself in, and resolves to take her own life immediately. She makes the Chorus swear they will withhold what they know from Theseus and hints that her death will have serious consequences for Hippolytus.

SECOND *STASIMON* (709–46)

As Phaedra prepares to end her life, the Chorus sing of their longing to escape to the fabled land of the Hesperides. They reflect on the ill-fated journey of Phaedra from Crete to Athens' shores.

THIRD EPISODE (747–1092)

A voice within announces that Phaedra has just hanged herself. The Chorus are reluctant to help. Theseus returns from the oracle, garlanded. He learns of Phaedra's death and laments. He then discovers a writing tablet in which Phaedra claims that Hippolytus has raped her. Horrified and enraged, Theseus employs one of three curses granted him by his father, Poseidon, and in addition banishes Hippolytus from Trozen and Athens.

Hippolytus enters. He has heard his father's lamentations and is astonished to find Phaedra's dead body. Theseus is unconvinced by his son's reaction and reflects bitterly on the deceitful nature of man. He then launches into a speech of condemnation, accusing Hippolytus of being a charlatan who uses the appearance of virtue to conceal wickedness. Hippolytus, bound by his oath to the Nurse, gives assurances of his good character and a solemn oath protesting his innocence. His speech has little impact on Theseus, who remains convinced by the testimony of his dead wife. Hippolytus bids farewell to Trozen and Athens and leaves to begin his exile.

THIRD *STASIMON* (1093–1132)

The Chorus consider the fickle nature of human affairs. They lament Hippolytus' exile and reflect on the injustice of the gods.

FOURTH EPISODE (1133–1242)

The Messenger enters and reports that Hippolytus has been fatally wounded as a consequence of Theseus' curse. He describes the crowd of friends who accompanied Hippolytus north of Trozen, along the shore of the Saronic Gulf; how suddenly a huge wave reared up and out of it came a savage bull which chased Hippolytus' chariot until it crashed. The team of horses dragged Hippolytus along the shore, dashing him against the rocks.

Theseus orders the Messenger to summon the dying Hippolytus.

FOURTH *STASIMON* (1243–58)

The Chorus sing a short ode to Eros and Aphrodite in which they reiterate the power these divinities have over all living things.

EXODOS (1259–1452)

Artemis appears *ex machina*. She reveals the truth of Phaedra's death to Theseus and condemns his hasty action against his son, although she also explains that Theseus' guilt is not absolute as he was simply carrying out Aphrodite's will.

Hippolytus is then brought on stage. In intense agony he laments his unfair fate, calling upon Zeus to witness the destruction of an innocent man. Artemis explains the role Aphrodite played in what has happened and Hippolytus comes to understand that her anger towards him has caused his misfortune. Artemis ends by predicting that Hippolytus will be worshipped by unmarried girls on the eve of their weddings and that Phaedra's love for him will always be remembered. She advises father and son to be reconciled.

Hippolytus forgives Theseus for his role in events and Theseus acknowledges the nobility of his illegitimate son. Hippolytus dies.

Pronunciation of names

To attempt the authentic pronunciation of classical Greek names presents great difficulties. It is perhaps easiest to accept the conventional anglicised versions of the familiar names (e.g. Ares, Zeus). The key below offers help with all the names in the play, which will give a reasonable overall consistency. Note that the main stress occurs on the italicised syllable.

KEY

ay—as in 'hay'	*ch*—as in Scottish 'loch'
ē—as in 'hair'	*i*—as in 'die'
ō—long 'o', as in 'go'	

Alcmene	Alk-*mee*-nee	Hellas	*Hel*-las
Alpheus	Al-*fe*-us	Hesperides	Hes-*per*-i-dees
Aphaea	Af-*i*-a	Hippolytus	Hip-*pol*-i-tus
Aphrodite	Af-ro-*di*-tee	Leto	*Lay*-tō
Apollo	A-*pol*-lō	Minos	*Mi*-nos
Argos	*Ar*-gos	Mounichus	*Moo*-ni-chus
Artemis	*Ar*-te-mis	Oceanus	Ō-kay-*ah*-nus
Asclepius	As-*klee*-pi-us	Oechalia	Oi-*cha*-li-a
Atlas	*At*-las	Olympus	Ol-*im*-pus
Bacchus	*Bak*-chus	Orpheus	Or-*fe*-us
Cecrops	*Ke*-krops	Pallantides	Pal-*lan*-ti-des
Cephalus	Ke-*fa*-lus	Pallas	*Pal*-las
Corybantes	Ko-ri-*ban*-tes	Pan	Pan
Crete	Kreet	Pandion	*Pan*-dee-on
Cypris	Ki-pris	Pelops	*Pe*-lops
Demeter	De-*mee*-ter	Phaedra	*Fi*-dra
Dictynna	Dik-*tin*-na	Phaethon	*Fi*-thōn
Dionysus	Di-o-*ni*-sus	Pittheus	*Pit*-the-us
Dirce	*Dur*-see	Poseidon	Po-*si*-dōn
Epidaurus	Ep-i-*dau*-rus	Sciron	*Ski*-rōn
Erechtheus	E-*rech*-thyus	Semele	*Se*-me-lee
Eridanus	E-*ri*-da-nus	Sinis	*Si*-nis
Eros	*Eer*-os	Thebes	Theebs
Eurytus	Yu-*ri*-tus	Theseus	*Thee*-dsyus
Hades	*Hay*-dees	Trozen	*Trō*-dzen
Hecate	*He*-ka-tee	Venetia	Ve-*nee*-sha
Helios	*Hee*-li-os	Zeus	Zyoos

Introduction to the Greek Theatre

Theātron, the Greek word that gave us 'theatre' in English, meant both 'viewing place' and the assembled viewers. These ancient viewers (*theātai*) were in some ways very different from their modern counterparts. For a start, they were participants in a religious festival, and they went to watch plays only on certain days in the year, when shows were put on in honour of Dionysus. At Athens, where drama developed many of its most significant traditions, the main Dionysus festival, held in the spring, was one of the most important events in the city's calendar, attracting large numbers of citizens and visitors from elsewhere in the Greek world. It is not known for certain whether women attended; if any did, they were more likely to be visitors than the wives of Athenian citizens.

The festival was also a great sporting occasion. Performances designed to win the god's favour needed spectators to witness and share in the event, just as the athletic contests did at Olympia or Delphi, and one of the ways in which the spectators got involved was through competition. What they saw were three sets of three tragedies plus a satyr-play, five separate comedies and as many as twenty song-and-dance performances called dithyrambs, put on in honour of Dionysus by choruses representing the different 'tribes' into which the citizen body was divided. There was a contest for each different event, with the dithyramb choruses divided into men's and boys' competitions, and a panel of judges determined the winners. The judges were appointed to act on behalf of the city; no doubt they took some notice of the way the audience responded on each occasion. Attendance at these events was on a large scale: we should be thinking of football crowds rather than typical theatre audiences in the modern world.

Like football matches, dramatic festivals were open-air occasions, and the performances were put on in daylight rather than with stage lighting in a darkened auditorium. The ideal performance space in these circumstances was a hollow hillside to seat spectators, with a flat area at the bottom (*orchēstra*) in which the chorusmen could spread out for their dancing and singing and which could be closed off by a stage-building (*skēnē*) acting simultaneously as backdrop, changing room and sounding board. Effective acoustics and good sight-lines were achieved by the kind of design represented in Fig. A on page 123, the theatre of Dionysus at Athens. The famous stone theatre at Epidaurus (Fig. B), built about 330 BC, and often taken as typical, has a circular *orchēstra*, but in the fifth century it was normal practice for theatres to have a low wooden stage in front of the *skēnē*, for use by the actors, who also interacted with the chorus in the *orchēstra*.

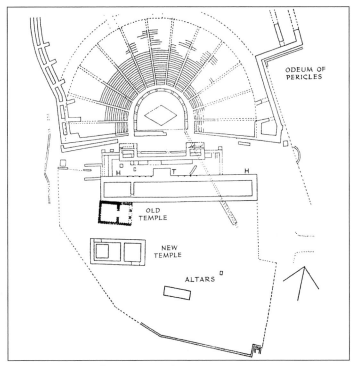

Fig. A. The theatre of Dionysus at Athens.

ODEUM OF
PERICLES

OLD
TEMPLE

NEW
TEMPLE

ALTARS

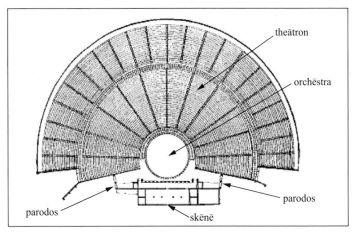

theātron

orchēstra

parodos

parodos

skēnē

Fig. B. The theatre at Epidaurus (fourth century BC).

Song and dance by choruses and the accompanying music of the piper were integral to all these types of performance and not just to the dithyramb. In tragedy there were 12 (later 15) chorusmen, in comedy 24, and in dithyramb 50; plays were often named after their chorus: Aeschylus' *Persians*, Euripides' *Bacchae* and Aristophanes' *Birds* are familiar examples. The rhythmic movements, groupings and singing of the chorus contributed crucially to the overall impact of each show, ensuring that there was always an animated stage picture even when only one or two actors were in view. The practice of keeping the number of speaking actors normally restricted to three, with doubling of roles by the same actor where necessary, looks odd at first sight, but it makes sense in the special circumstance of Greek theatrical performance. Two factors are particularly relevant: first the use of masks, which was probably felt to be fundamental to shows associated with the cult of Dionysus and which made it easy for an actor to take more than one part within a single play, and second the need to concentrate the audience's attention by keeping the number of possible speakers limited. In a large, open acting area some kind of focusing device is important if the spectators are always to be sure where to direct their gaze. The Greek plays that have survived, particularly the tragedies, are extremely economical in their design, with no sub-plots or complications in the action which audiences might find distracting or confusing. Acting style, too, seems to have relied on large gestures and avoidance of fussy detail; we know from the size of some of the surviving theatres that many spectators would be sitting too far away to catch small-scale gestures or stage business. Some plays make powerful use of props, like Ajax's sword, Philoctetes' bow, or the head of Pentheus in *Bacchae*, but all these are carefully chosen to be easily seen and interpreted.

Above all, actors seem to have depended on their highly trained voices in order to captivate audiences and stir their emotions. By the middle of the fifth century there was a prize for the best actor in the tragic competition, as well as for the playwright and the financial sponsor of the performance (*chorēgos*), and comedy followed suit a little later. What was most admired in the leading actors who were entitled to compete for this prize was the ability to play a series of different and very demanding parts in a single day and to be a brilliant singer as well as a compelling speaker of verse: many of the main parts involve solo songs or complex exchanges between actor and chorus. Overall, the best plays and performances must have offered audiences a great charge of energy and excitement: the chance to see a group of chorusmen dancing and singing in a sequence of different guises, as young maidens, old counsellors, ecstatic maenads, and exuberant satyrs; to watch scenes in which supernatural beings – gods, Furies, ghosts – come into contact with human beings; to listen to intense debates and hear the blood-curdling offstage cries that heralded the arrival of a messenger with an account of terrifying deeds within, and then to see the bodies brought out and witness the lamentations. Far more 'happened' in most plays than we can easily imagine from the bare text on the page; this must help to account for the continuing appeal of drama throughout antiquity and across the Greco-Roman world.

From the fourth century onwards dramatic festivals became popular wherever there were communities of Greek speakers, and other gods besides Dionysus were honoured with performances of plays. Actors, dancers and musicians organised themselves for professional touring – some of them achieved star status and earned huge fees – and famous old plays were revived as part of the repertoire. Some of the plays that had been first performed for Athenian citizens in the fifth century became classics for very different audiences – women as well as men, Latin speakers as well as Greeks – and took on new kinds of meaning in their new environment. But theatre was very far from being an antiquarian institution: new plays, new dramatic forms like mime and pantomime, changes in theatre design, staging, masks and costumes all demonstrate its continuing vitality in the Hellenistic and Roman periods. Nearly all the Greek plays that have survived into modern times are ones that had a long theatrical life in antiquity; this perhaps helps to explain why modern actors, directors and audiences have been able to rediscover their power.

For further reading: entries in *Oxford Classical Dictionary* (3rd edition) under 'theatre staging, Greek' and 'tragedy, Greek'; J.R. Green, 'The theatre', Ch. 7 of *The Cambridge Ancient History, Plates to Volumes V and VI*, Cambridge, 1994; Richard Green and Eric Handley, *Images of the Greek Theatre*, London, 1995; Rush Rehm, *Greek Tragic Theatre*, London and New York, 1992; P.E. Easterling (ed.), *The Cambridge Companion to Greek Tragedy*, Cambridge, 1997; David Wiles, *Tragedy in Athens*, Cambridge, 1997.

Pat Easterling

Time line

Dates of selected authors and extant works

12th century BC	**The Trojan war**	
8th century BC	**HOMER**	• *The Iliad* • *The Odyssey*
5th century BC 490–479 431–404	**The Persian wars** **The Peloponnesian wars**	

c. 525/4–456/5
 	
472
 	
456
	AESCHYLUS	(In probable order.)
		
		• *Persians*
		• *Seven against Thebes*
		• *Suppliants*
		• ***Oresteia Trilogy:***
		   Agamemnon, Choephoroi
		   Eumenides
		• *Prometheus Bound*

c. 496/5–406 409 401 (posthumous)	**SOPHOCLES**	(Undated plays are in alphabetical order.) • *Ajax* • *Oedipus Tyrannus* • *Antigone* • *Trachiniae* • *Electra* • *Philoctetes* • *Oedipus at Colonus*
c. 490/80–407/6 438 (1st production 455) 431 428 415 412 409 ?408 ?408–6	**EURIPIDES**	(In probable order.) • *Alcestis* • *Medea* • *Heracleidae* • *Hippolytus* • *Andromache* • *Hecuba* • *Suppliant Women* • *Electra* • *Trojan Women* • *Heracles* • *Iphigenia among the Taurians* • *Helen* • *Ion* • *Phoenissae* • *Orestes* • *Cyclops* (satyr-play) • *Bacchae* • *Iphigenia at Aulis*
460/50–*c.* 386 411 405	**ARISTOPHANES**	(Selected works.) • *Thesmophoriazusae* • *Lysistrata* • *Frogs*
4th century BC 384–322	**ARISTOTLE**	(Selected works.) • *The Art of Poetry*

Index

Bold numbers refer to pages. Other numbers are line references.